Praise for *I*

"Sharp and honest, deep and convincing, *Necessary Risks* offers a way through fear and risk toward addressing one of the most intractable questions of our day: systemic racism. It's rare that a book can both diagnose a problem and provide the visceral hope of lived experience. Ott's journey through her own privilege invites others to consider both their privilege and their power to effect change."

—Amy Frykholm, senior editor, *The Christian Century*; author of *Wild Woman: A Footnote, the Desert, and My Quest for an Elusive Saint*

"What a gift it has been to read Teri McDowell Ott's *Necessary Risks: Challenges Privileged People Need to Face*. Written with laser-sharp clarity, grounded in compelling research, and infused with disarming humor and honest vulnerability, the book stopped me in my tracks again and again, exposing the blindness of my own privilege. Perhaps more importantly, though, Ott's book took me by the hand to invite me out of privileged paralysis and awakened a kaleidoscope of possibilities that we actually can do something."

—Mark DeVries, founder of Ministry Architects and cofounder of Ministry Incubators

"If you read and ponder Teri McDowell Ott's remarkable book, as I just did, it could change your life. Through her determined personal experiences, including visiting and listening to Black men in a prison and to women of color in her mostly White college, she traces her own process of coming to terms with her White privilege, which was slow in spite of her progressive, inclusive intent. It is perhaps the hardest, but also most important, lesson for all of us to learn. Along the way, Ott provides a very helpful list of books White people concerned with cultural racism should read and suggests action steps at the end of each chapter. I'm so glad I read this book. You will be too."

—John M. Buchanan, pastor emeritus, Fourth Presbyterian Church of Chicago, and former editor/publisher, *The Christian Century*

"The only risk is not moving, not trying, not succeeding, not relating, and not belonging in the struggle for justice, equity, and love. Teri McDowell Ott provides the pragmatic, daily guidance that can help people bring about a more equitable and inclusive society. It is a necessary and faithful reframing of the risk for 'White privileged souls.' In short, they risk their own futures if they do not create conditions for BIPOC and other marginalized communities to thrive."

—Patrick B. Reyes, author of *The Purpose Gap*

"Teri McDowell Ott's *Necessary Risks* is a wonderful, systematic, and practical introduction to the soul-saving work that privileged White Christians who take Jesus seriously must do. Book and Bible-study groups and courageous preachers will find in this text a conversion guide that helps them and the Holy Spirit do the work that one's soul must do."

—Angela Cowser, associate professor of Black church studies and associate dean of Black church studies and doctor of ministry programs at Louisville Presbyterian Theological Seminary; pastor in the Presbyterian Church (U.S.A.); organizer with the Industrial Areas Foundation

"Teri McDowell Ott takes a tremendous risk in challenging each of us to be better, to do more, and to risk learning from one other. Her book is not a condemnation of whites but an attempt to better understand the connection between race and struggle. She insightfully defines 'white privilege' as real and intimately connected to race. Her ten risks encourage us to go to uncomfortable places, to stay and learn, to teach others while following the lead of impacted persons, and not to fear either failing or succeeding. It is indeed an 'invitation for privileged people to move beyond fear, to take necessary risks, to heal and free our souls. The struggle is life and life-giving.' She invites us on a journey knowing that we do not travel alone, and that together we can go far."

—Jimmie R. Hawkins, director of the Presbyterian Church (U.S.A.) Advocacy Offices, Office of Public Witness and Ministry at the United Nations

"*Necessary Risks* challenges the reader through a personal narrative filled with stories, resources, and thought-provoking reflective activities at the end of each chapter. Readers will recognize and relate to the stories and will learn to move beyond the fear, take risks, and move the racial conversation forward."

—Eddie Moore Jr., PhD, founder and program director, The White Privilege Conference

Necessary Risks

Necessary Risks

Challenges Privileged
People Need to Face

Teri McDowell Ott

Fortress Press

Minneapolis

NECESSARY RISKS
Challenges Privileged People Need to Face

Scripture quotations are from the New Revised Standard Version
Bible © 1989 Division of Christian Education of the National Council
of the Churches of Christ in the United States of America. Used by
permission.

Cover Photo: Lagui, Masterfile.com/400-05039956
Cover Design: John M. Lucas

Print ISBN: 978-1-5064-7181-5
eBook ISBN: 978-1-5064-7182-2

For Dan, my husband and best friend

For Isaac and Ella, my inspiration

Contents

Preface

W riting is the way I make sense of the world. It's my spiritual practice of weaving thoughts, feelings, personal experiences, and what I'm currently reading together on the page. Writing is also how I push myself to grow and mature, a moral practice of raising myself to a new consciousness. My hope in publishing a book like this is that it can also serve as a spiritual and moral practice for readers.

Whenever personal experiences are published, a writer must make choices about what is revealed, how the story should be told, who should be named, and who should be kept anonymous. I always try to be as honest as possible in my writing, but transparency is not a virtue of America's carceral system. In writing about my experiences as a volunteer in a men's prison, I have had to disguise the identity of the incarcerated men, the facility, and the staff. It pains me not to name and acknowledge the incarcerated men from whom I have learned so much. Their voices deserve to be heard. Their agency should not be denied. America incarcerates more brothers, sisters, mothers, fathers, sons, and daughters than any other country—approximately 2.3 million people whose stories are kept from us by a dehumanizing criminal justice system. There is a jail or a prison near every American town. I hope readers of this book might be inspired to volunteer in a jail or a prison themselves to get to know, by name, the people we have locked away.

For purposes of confidentiality, I have also changed the names of the college students I refer to in this book. Whenever possible, I have shown students what I have written about them to ask if I have gotten the story correct and if they were uncomfortable with anything I wrote.

I use the term *marginalized* in this book instead of *minority*. The term *minority* conveys that a person's identity is encapsulated in being less than the majority. *Marginalized* more appropriately reflects how groups of people have been acted upon or pushed to the margins of society by people with power and privilege, usually the majority. This is also why I refer to the men I have met in prison as *incarcerated*, as opposed to *prisoners*, *felons*, or *inmates*, because these men are more than the crimes for which they have been convicted.

Finally, I capitalize White, Black, and Brown in reference to race. I made this change in my writing after learning that this is currently the preference of Black and Brown people, that the capitalization emphasizes the particularity of racial experience. I also believe it's important for White people to acknowledge that we, too, have a particular racial experience and culture. White does not (or should not) represent a neutral standard; rather, it is one particularity among many. This preference for capitalization may change by the time the book is published. If it does, I'll adjust my future writing, because it is important to listen to and respect the way people, particularly marginalized people, prefer to be identified.

Acknowledgments

My writing journey has been blessed by many whom I wish to gratefully acknowledge. Barb McCarty Clauer, my college roommate, first got me journaling. William Palmer, my college professor, cheered on my creative writing with green asterisks next to clever turns of phrase. Christine Hemp, poet and teacher extraordinaire, believed in me and coached me into my first publishing breakthroughs. Steve Thorngate and Amy Frykholm at the *Christian Century* first published my writing and honed my skill with their wise and faithful editing (portions of this book were originally published in the *Christian Century*). Valerie Weaver-Zercher gave me the idea to structure this book around risk. Beth Gaede, my editor at Fortress Press, has been patient and persistent and believed in this book from the start. My incredible clergy women's writing group—Melissa Earley, Heidi Haverkamp, Celeste Kennel-Shank, Meghan Murphy-Gill, and Elizabeth Felicetti—are always ready to celebrate, encourage, and receive a rant. Allison K. Williams has accompanied this book through its many proposals and countless chapter drafts—I would not be where I am today without her exceptional advice, talent, editing prowess, and much-needed pep talks. The faculty, staff, and students of

Preface

Monmouth College—particularly Jocelyn—challenged me and led me to learn and grow. The board of *Presbyterian Outlook* trusted a small-town college chaplain to become their new editor. The incarcerated men I have met and gotten to know have been my constant inspiration. My parents, Tom and Sue McDowell, have always loved and supported me and raised me in a church that taught me loving God meant loving my neighbor.

Introduction
On Fear

In my adult life I have seen few white folks who are really willing to go the distance to create a world of racial equity—white folks willing to take risks, to be courageous, to live against the grain.

—bell hooks, *Teaching to Transgress*

I t was a beautiful midwestern fall day, with sunlight streaming through the decorative stained-glass frame I had perched in my office window. Alma and Kyra didn't notice the sun, though, or the rosy glow cast by the stained glass. They sat close together on the other side of the table from me, exchanging glances every now and then as we talked. My two student interns and I were working on an educational program to communicate marginalized students' concerns to faculty and staff: Ten Things We Want You to Know.

In preparation for the program, Alma and Kyra had visited with and surveyed groups of marginalized students on our campus and asked them, "What would you want the faculty and staff to know about your college experience?" Today, we were meeting to cull and compile all of the feedback they'd received into our list. A few of the "things" that made the list:

> Code-switching is survival for me.
> I overhear things on campus that make me feel unsafe.
> If I start to share my feelings or experience, I don't need you to save me; I just need to be heard.

As they shared the collected students' feedback, I asked questions to clarify and define the concerns the marginalized students were trying to get across: "Can you tell me more about how it feels to have to code-switch?" "Can you share an example or a story of when you felt unsafe on campus?" Alma and Kyra paused after each question, sometimes looking up at the ceiling or closing their eyes. They were working hard to respond to my questions, trying to teach a White woman what it's like to be a Black or Latinx or LGBTQ+ student at our small, private liberal arts college.

We spent the most time teasing out a point about the unique mental health issues of marginalized students that Kyra, in particular, felt was important to share. I'd heard other Black students tell me their parents didn't support their need for counseling or for antidepressants. This lack of mental health support didn't surprise me. Mental illness has only recently begun to be destigmatized. But Kyra was trying to articulate something more, something specific to her Black experience. After going around and around on this topic, with me asking question after question trying to understand, Kyra finally broke through my confusion, saying, "At home, I'm told, 'You're not depressed; you're just Black.' So it's really hard to differentiate between my struggle as a person of color and my struggle with depression."

I asked more questions, encouraging them to clarify and articulate what they knew was true but had not spoken out loud or tried to explain before to someone whose experience was vastly different from their own.

Finally, after about an hour of this draining work, Kyra paused, smiled shyly, and confessed, "I'm scared."

"Yeah. Me too," Alma added.

I thought I understood. Here were two college students working on a program to teach their teachers. The pressure to do this program right, to perform well, felt intense. I impulsively jumped to comfort them.

"Honestly, I'm scared too," I shared. "But I've also come to recognize that if I'm scared to do something, it's usually worth doing—that there's something meaningful, something good on the other side of that fear."

Alma and Kyra nodded. What I said seemed to resonate. They wanted to lead this program in spite of their fear.

Fear has always been my nemesis. My childhood was shaped by a painful shyness, panic attacks, and irrational phobias. Too afraid to raise my hand and call attention to myself in elementary school, I peed my pants and sat the class out in a puddle of shame. Fearing the embarrassment of falling asleep in my high school classes, I'd go to bed hours early, toss and turn, then work myself into a panicked fit that would keep me awake later than if I'd gone to bed on time. It would be decades before I learned that the overwhelming emotions I experienced before a big sporting event, or a required speech at school, or at night while trying to go to sleep were panic attacks that I would eventually learn to manage. Until I learned this, though, I was a mess—an awkward, insecure girl whose fear dictated and controlled her life.

An experience during my junior year of college changed my course. One evening, I sat cross-legged on the navy-blue bedspread of my dorm mattress reading a book that I was too embarrassed to tell anyone about—some light fiction about a modern-day Jesus. I'd always been interested in religion and was raised in the Presbyterian Church. But I didn't want anyone to think I was *religious* or some sort of "Jesus freak," so I kept my faith to myself.

The book was open and turned upside down against my bedspread's pattern of tiny pink roses. My face in my hands, I sobbed and heaved for air, overcome by what I had just read. I can't remember the exact text, just the recognition, the feeling, the sudden knowing that God wanted more from me and for me than the life I imagined for myself.

I had started to come out of my shy shell in college, but not enough to take Jesus seriously when he first suggested I follow him to seminary. Oh, Jesus, what a riot. He had to be joking, right?

Introduction

Nope.

My Presbyterian Church background led me to assume that people who go to seminary have to become pastors who don long black robes and speak with moral gravitas from tall pulpits. At that point in my life, I was still afraid to speak to boys.

I fought Jesus hard, doubting that I had what it took to be any kind of religious leader. But Jesus was relentless. In the days that followed, I couldn't stop thinking about seminary. I was scared but also curious, wondering what it would be like, wondering what I might be like in that new space. Jesus didn't allow me any relief—no excuse was good enough. The negotiations were difficult and fraught, and in the end, my twenty-year-old self issued an ultimatum that felt reasonable: "OK, Jesus, I'll do this one thing. I'll go to seminary. But don't expect much more than that. Don't expect me to be someone I'm not or become some kind of pastor who speaks, out loud, in front of people. I'm just going to go, take some classes, then get back to my life. OK? OK."

Jesus didn't respond. Sigh.

As it turned out, seminary was the right move. I loved studying Scripture and theology and pastoral counseling. But when I was called to speak in class or invited to preach from an actual pulpit, my fear took over, and I panicked. In these agonizing moments, I'd pray desperate prayers and get frank with God. "What the hell were you thinking?" I'd accuse the One who I believed got me into this mess. "Why couldn't you have called me to some quiet cubicle somewhere?"

God doesn't help my anxiety much in these fear-filled moments. Cortisol rushes to my brain, and the Holy Spirit doesn't come in an antidepressant form. What did help was a growing impatience with having spent too much of my life in hiding. I wanted out. I wanted to be liberated from the fears that kept me captive.

In my studies, I discovered feminist theologian Susan Nelson Dunfee's classic article "The Sin of Hiding," which critiques Reinhold Niebuhr's doctrine of sin. Niebuhr emphasizes pride as the primary sin and promotes self-sacrifice as the way to self-transcendence. Nelson Dunfee argues that this approach negates what she sees as the primary sin of woman: the sin of *hiding*. In order for a woman to know self-transcendence—to know her full humanity—she must confess to the sin of hiding, stand "exposed in her insecurities and self-doubts, revealed in her true vulnerability, so she can learn how to cope either with her own shortcomings, or with her talents and desires." In this way, "the woman is on the record; she is given a forum, an arena, a *life* to be lived."[1]

Nelson Dunfee's words resonated deeply with me. Since then, I have been slowly untangling myself from all that has kept me in hiding. As a young seminarian, it was hard to ignore the voices in my head saying that I didn't have much to give—that I certainly didn't have anything to say worthy of a pulpit. Even now, I am still learning to trust the people who encourage me—and the call that keeps urging me out of hiding toward more.

In his book *Be Still and Get Going: A Jewish Meditation Practice for Real Life*, Rabbi Alan Lew shares the two different words for fear used in the Hebrew Bible. *Pachad*, Lew explains, is imagined or projected fear, being afraid of something we think might happen but likely won't. *Pachad* describes the irrational worst-case scenarios we conjure, like my nightmares about people laughing and mocking me as I preach.

According to Lew, the second Hebrew word for fear is *norah*. This is the fear we experience when we come into the presence of the Divine. The book of Psalms frequently refers to this fear as the appropriate way to approach and be in relationship with God: "Happy are those who fear the Lord" (Ps 112:1). "The fear of the Lord is the beginning of wisdom" (Ps 111:10). But Lew also explains *norah* as the fear that overcomes us when we find ourselves in a larger space than we are used to or experiencing an energy we hadn't felt before. *Norah* is what we feel when we come out of hiding, laying ourselves bare to the moment, the opportunity, the experience of being more and being in the presence of More.

All the time I've spent trying to manage my fear, I never considered it to have any redeeming value. Fear is the most uncomfortable of emotions. One we go to great lengths to avoid—numbing ourselves with alcohol, stockpiling guns, building walls and fences to keep the "scary" out. Feeling safe and secure is a privilege. I've learned this from my students who live in neighborhoods with higher crime on Chicago's South Side. They live in fear of real danger: the fear of getting shot on their walk home from school or the fear of police stopping them and then pinning them to the sidewalk on their way to the corner store to fetch milk for dinner.

No matter how we seek to protect or secure ourselves, fear is unavoidable. It is an elemental part of being human that should be better understood and often embraced. The tension or discomfort of fear can lead us to transformation and growth.

In his essay "Antidotes to Fear," Martin Luther King Jr. describes how necessary fear is to the human experience:

> Fear is the elemental alarm system of the human organism which warns of approaching dangers and without which man could not have survived in either the primitive or modern world. Fear, moreover, is a powerfully creative force. Every great invention and intellectual advance represents a desire to escape from some dreaded circumstance or condition. The fear of darkness led to the discovery of the secret of electricity. The fear of pain led to the marvelous advances of medical science. The fear of ignorance was one reason that man built great institutions of learning. The fear of war was one of the forces behind the birth of the United Nations. If man were to lose his capacity to fear, he would be deprived of his capacity to grow, invent and create.[2]

My first sermon took me six months to write and eight minutes to deliver, and it left the muscles in my neck and back so stiff, I thought the congregation was going to have to prop me up on a backboard. But I did it. And then I did it again. Those early sermons weren't great. But in time and with practice, they got better.

After seminary, I went on to serve three churches in pastoral positions where preaching was a regular part of the job. In any form, public speaking's not easy for me. Xanax is still my best friend in the pulpit. But the more I speak, the more I push myself out of hiding and into the larger space of *norah*, the more I become who I am meant to be.

By the time I met with Alma and Kyra, I had come to recognize my fear as a sign, a signal flare that what I was afraid of doing was worth doing. Fear had caged and kept me from a lot of early growth and development. Once I found the courage to take some risks, I found the path to freedom—the path to liberate my thinking, my growth, my creativity, my human potential. I wanted Alma and Kyra to know this liberation too.

But the more I contemplated the advice I gave them, the more I wondered if it was appropriate. Kyra is an African American. Alma is a Deferred Action for Childhood Arrivals (DACA) student whose family emigrated from Mexico. The more I have learned about the lives of my marginalized students, the more I realize that what we fear and what we face are not the same.

In his powerful book *My Grandmother's Hands: Racialized Trauma and the Pathway to Mending Our Hearts and Bodies*, Resmaa Menakem describes the embodied fear Black and White people hold for each other. In 1619, when Africans were first brought to our continent as slaves, through the 1690s, when race was constructed as a legal and easy way to distinguish who was free and who was not, a system of domination was institutionalized that would traumatize both oppressor and oppressed.

"Trauma," Menakem writes, "is not an event. It is not a flaw or a weakness. It is a highly effective tool of safety and survival. Trauma is the body's protective response to an event—or a series of events—that it perceives as potentially dangerous."[3] Our embedded trauma response is fight, flee, or freeze, triggered by what neuroscientists call our vagus nerve, or what we might refer to as our lizard brain, because it reacts before we can think.

In the aftermath of a highly stressful event, Menakem explains, our vagus nerve may embed a reflexive trauma response, or a wordless story of danger, in our body. This embodied story is routinely passed from person to person and generation to generation through inherited genetics, culture, and family structures. If the trauma is not addressed and the pain not metabolized and healed, the result is what therapists call traumatic retention, an embodiment of violence and abuse that gets so internalized within a particular group of people that it can begin to simply look like that group's culture—their way of being and behaving—not a survival response to repeatedly triggered trauma.

According to Kyra's community, being Black means being depressed. The trauma Black people embody has become so internalized, so normalized, that persistent sadness is simply (and tragically) accepted as a part of Black culture.

Menakem's grandmother, whose hands were large and swollen from her childhood cotton picking, inspired his work on embodied trauma. He observed how she would rock herself and hum in order to settle her nerves. "The trauma that lives in Black bodies is deep and persistent," Menakem writes.[4] Many Black bodies cannot feel settled around White ones. Over generations, African Americans have developed a variety of physical practices and rituals that help them settle, such as humming, rocking, rhythmic clapping, drumming, and singing.

Reading Menakem, I often thought of Alma and Kyra, huddled together on the other side of my small office table. If they'd felt safe enough to physically hug and rock each other in that moment, I think they would have. They were trying to be brave in spite of their nerves and their embedded stories of danger telling them to fight, flee, or freeze. Their fear of leading a group of faculty and staff, a group of predominantly White people with more privilege and power than they will likely ever know, is not the same as mine.

My White body also knows generational racialized trauma, embedded within me by witnessing and benefiting from Whites' historical dehumanization of Black bodies. My fight, flee, or freeze response is triggered by fabricated stories of danger, created by White people to justify Black enslavement and oppression—the myth that the Black body is dangerous, impervious to pain, even monstrous. The myth that White bodies are vulnerable and fragile in comparison to Black bodies and so must be protected and defended from them.

Menakem refers to our racialized trauma as a "soul wound." It is a wounding of what makes us fundamentally human. A wounding of our ability to move beyond animalistic, lizard instincts to a liberating path of healing and freeing ourselves from our racialized trauma and preventing its perpetuation. How painful it is to face this soul wound, to face our trauma, our brokenness, our spiritual and moral failings. How fearful it is to come out of hiding, lay ourselves bare to our suffering and the suffering of others, and risk being and becoming more. But it is our path to liberation. It is a risk worth taking.

"In my adult life," writes bell hooks, "I have seen few white folks who are really willing to go the distance to create a world of racial equity—white folks willing to take risks, to be courageous, to live against the grain."[5]

My hope for this book is that it inspires more White privileged people like me to take risks, to be courageous, to face our fears and move forward in learning, growth, and transformation. I define *privilege* as an unearned advantage that might or might not include inherited wealth, networks, and connections. Conservatives have argued that racial privilege doesn't exist—that poor Whites and people of color who work hard and achieve economic success prove this. But I still believe privilege is connected to race because I recognize the unearned advantages my Whiteness affords: immunity from being racially profiled when pulled over by the police or followed like a suspect while shopping in a store. I've read about Black parents giving their children White names so their résumés will more likely be considered. "White privilege" doesn't negate or "cancel" how hard White people have worked for what they have or the circumstances with which they have struggled. It does mean their struggle isn't tied to their race.

Through these chapters, I will follow a variety of Black, Latinx, and Queer liberationists, people whose extraordinary wisdom emanates from their fearless commitment to face their soul wounds and ours. I hope this book helps readers discern what risks they can and should take. If the benefits and comfort of racial privilege come at the expense of caging ourselves and our souls in dehumanizing systems, it is worth it to "go the distance" for racial equity. Our White privileged souls are as much at stake as those who are less privileged. Our wounds, our historically retained trauma, are as much in need of healing. This is the hard and necessary work we must risk to liberate us all.

Chapter One

Risk Going

At some point, on our way to a new consciousness, we
will have to leave the opposite bank . . . cross the border
into a wholly new and separate territory.

—GLORIA ANZALDÚA, *Borderlands/
La Frontera: The New Mestiza*

DO NOT PICK UP HITCHHIKERS.

F or six years, I read this sign as I drove by the barbed wire–
topped fencing of the prison, the sniper towers and sta-
dium lights, the men exercising in the yard along the highway.

I'm too busy to get involved at that prison, I told myself. *I'm a
mom of young kids, a wife, a college chaplain, and a volunteer already.*

The men wore white tank tops and blue pants and
appeared to congregate by race—Whites lifting weights or

jogging, Black players on the basketball court, Latino men playing soccer. Twenty-four years ago in Clarion, Illinois, nobody wanted these men as neighbors. The governor said the prison was necessary to get dangerous criminals off the streets. Prisons were being built all over the state, he said. They were a boon to the economy, a source of jobs. The community protested. The governor got his way. The prison was built to incarcerate nine hundred men at medium security. Today, there are over eighteen hundred men up to maximum security.

I'm doing enough. I'd led studies of mass incarceration and Michelle Alexander's *The New Jim Crow.* I'd taken students to Washington, DC, to observe programs for ex-felons and to argue for criminal justice reform.

The need would overwhelm me.

In seminary, I volunteered for a pastoral counseling practicum at a women's prison. I met with two women who spoke about survival on the streets, getting involved with gangs for protection, support, belonging, and ultimately crime. Drugs and addiction felt like an inevitable path in their neighborhood. I wondered what separated me from them. My zip code? My family? My Whiteness? My sheltered existence exposed, I struggled with questions like "Why them? Why not me?" and finished the practicum wiser than I began.

But this is a men's prison. They probably wouldn't even let me in.

One bright spring day, after dropping my kids off at their elementary school nestled in the cornfields of west central Illinois, I checked the email on my phone. An article by prison chaplain Chris Hoke had landed in my feed. I'd recently heard

Chris speak at a conference. He was a great storyteller, truly inspiring. It was still early, and I didn't have anything pressing at the office, so I pulled into a quiet parking spot at the school and slumped down in the leather seat of my car to read:

> America leads the world in incarcerating its own people. Almost two and a half million human beings are locked away in mass social tombs, an overstuffed underground beneath our society. They are not physically dead like Lazarus, of course, but philosopher Lisa Guenther calls it "social death"—cut off from loved ones, family, and their children. Huge geographic distances, dozens of thick walls, and expensive phone calls seal these men and women off from the land of the living. They are effectively dead to society. What if every church wrote to, adopted, and received just one prisoner? Two things would happen. We would empty the prison system, and every church would be changed.[1]

Chris's challenge undid me.

I'm too busy.

My chest burned and my heart pounded as I placed my forehead on the steering wheel of my running car to try to get a grip.

I'm doing enough.

I knew this feeling. I'd felt it before when I had to overcome my own objections to go to seminary. I was being called or led or shoved in the direction of the prison.

The need would overwhelm me.

All of my excuses unraveled, none of them valid in the face of a faith that calls me to serve those whom society has left for dead.

"I'd really rather not," I said out loud to the One I believed was responsible for this. "That place scares me. And it's different from the time I visited a prison in seminary. There were only women there. It was part of a class. I was younger then. Besides, I've already followed You here to this college and this call to be a chaplain. That was hard enough. No family nearby to babysit when my kids get sick. No good sushi. What more do you expect of me?" Even as I prayed these words of protest, I knew I would never escape this relentless, unflagging feeling unless I followed where it led.

"OK, fine. I'll try," I prayed. "But if I get stabbed, it's on You."

✂

Of all the spaces I had feared going, the men's prison in Clarion was at the top of my list of scary places where Teri does not belong. But there are others. In my work as a college chaplain, I had feared approaching the Black students' table in the dining hall, the house where the international students hang out, a living room full of Latinas studying mujerista theology.

Simply put, there are some spaces where I feel like I, as a White woman of privilege, only intrude if I enter. In her book *Why Are All the Black Kids Sitting Together in the Cafeteria?*, Beverly Tatum describes the importance of positive group development and racial identity among youth of color. She explains how the Black students' table in the dining hall can serve as a source of psychological protection for Black youth who "from early childhood through preadolescent years are exposed to and absorb many of the beliefs and values of the dominant White culture, including the idea that Whites are the preferred group in US Society."[2] I understand the need for people of color to have their own space.

I am also cautioned by Shannon Sullivan's identification of a White racial assumption that "all cultural and social spaces are potentially available for us to inhabit."[3] White people, according to Sullivan, privilege themselves with an "ontological expansiveness," an understanding that we can move and expand into all spaces—that nowhere is off-limits. This is not true for people of color, and there are clear consequences when this racial contract is broken. An example is the killing of Ahmaud Arbery by two White men in Satilla Shores, Georgia. Arbery's only "transgression" was jogging through a White neighborhood as a Black man. News of the killing spread while Covid-19 stay-at-home orders were being protested by White people—some of whom stormed their state capitols with rifles—claiming their freedoms and their right to go wherever they pleased were being impinged.

The risk of going to another's cultural domain feels especially perilous because there are all sorts of ways for White privileged people to screw up. Our violent history of colonialism—or as our European ancestors would have called it, "civilizing wild people and wild places"—follows us into every new cultural setting. Our habits of acculturation, where "we take land, people, and the fruit of other's labor and creativity as our own,"[4] also haunt us. In fact, I've known people who have argued that we White people shouldn't go into the space of others because we are bound to get it wrong, to violate cultural sensitivities, to impose our ways on theirs.

But I am convicted by the words of Brazilian educator Paulo Freire that "solidarity requires that one enter into the situation of those with whom one is solidary."[5] The tension we experience in border crossings is real and can leave one paralyzed on the safe, known side, all too ready to accept every excuse for why we shouldn't take the risk. Staying safe on our "side," though, is not activism, and it is not what our society needs. As Bryan Stevenson, the author of *Just Mercy* and influential activist for criminal justice reform, writes, "You've got to get proximate to suffering and injustice. It's just not enough to buy a T-shirt or issue a tweet, and do some of the things that people sometimes do and confuse it for activism that makes a difference."[6]

The prison kept calling me.

"Parker Correctional, Pérez speaking."

"Oh, hi. Are you the chaplain?"

"Yes."

I shift in my office chair, my eyes searching the ceiling. "Well, I'm not really sure why I'm calling." Leaning over my desk, I put my forehead in my hand. "My name is Teri Ott. I'm the chaplain at the college down the road from you."

"Oh, yes. I know you." His tone is matter-of-fact.

"You know me?"

"Yes. I was at that wedding you officiated last summer. The Harry Potter wedding."

"What? Really?"

"Yes. I was wondering how you were going to pull that off."

I laugh. "Actually, it was OK, except for the creepy owl they perched behind my shoulder. Did you know the bride or the groom?"

"The groom," Chaplain Pérez answers. "He grew up in my church."

"That's crazy. This is crazy."

"So what can I do for you?"

The man on the other end of the phone has seen me officiate a wedding. He knows I am legitimate enough for that, so I venture into an explanation. "I've been driving by your prison for six years, and I see the men in the yard, and, well, the prison has just been calling to me. I drive by at least once a week."

I think maybe he will stop me from going any further—tell me women aren't allowed in the men's prison, tell me I shouldn't have even called. But he doesn't. He doesn't say anything at all.

"I'm superbusy, though. And it's a men's prison. And I don't really know what I could do. But yeah, that's why I'm calling."

Finally, he responds, in the same nothing-weird-about-this tone as before: "Why don't you come for a visit? Are you free on Thursday morning? Maybe 10:00 a.m.?"

"Oh. Hmm." *What have I just done?* "OK. I can do that. I can come on Thursday."

"Great. I'll see you then," Chaplain Pérez says. "Don't bring any electronics. No cell phone. No Fitbit."

"OK. I'll see you on Thursday."

That night, I dream a riot breaks out while I am visiting the prison.

❋

In her influential book *Borderlands / La Frontera: The New Mestiza*, Gloria Anzaldúa encourages readers to risk going, to venture into the borderlands—a place where different cultures meet and mix. To live in the borderlands, Anzaldúa writes, is to "put *chile* in the borscht, eat whole wheat tortillas, speak Tex-Mex with a Brooklyn accent." It's also a place, though, where you'll "be stopped by *la migra* [US Immigration and Customs Enforcement officers] at the border checkpoints."[7] The borderlands are a place of struggle, of growing identity awareness and new consciousness.

Anzaldúa's life is a story of struggling against profound oppression, sexism, and racism in her home of South Texas, her patriarchal Mexican culture, and an educational system that did not value her work in Chicana studies. In spite of these oppressive forces, Anzaldúa never hesitated to claim her Mexican, Chicana, and American identities. Her life and work modeled the philosophy espoused in *Borderlands / La Frontera*—"that it is possible to both understand and reject, to love and detest, to be loyal and question, and above all to continue to seek enlightenment out of the ambiguity and contradiction of all social existence."[8]

Anzaldúa specifically condemns the United States' dominant White culture, which, she writes, "is killing us slowly with its ignorance." One of the weapons White culture uses to dominate and control is separation—barricading others behind tribal walls so White elites can then "whitewash and distort history."[9] US history with Mexico illustrates this. In the 1800s, Whites illegally migrated into the part of Mexico that is now Texas. They violently and cruelly drove the natives from this land. In the 1836 Battle of the Alamo, Mexico's response to this invasion, Mexican forces reclaimed San Antonio's Alamo Mission and killed its occupants. This battle was used by White imperialists to inflame American prejudice of our southern neighbors, maligning Mexicans as a wicked and dangerous people and justifying more war and more violent colonizing of Mexican land.[10] In today's debate over Mexican immigration to the United States, White Americans do not acknowledge our role in this violent border history, whitewashing our culpability and maintaining a distorted prejudice of Mexicans as "dangerous" or "illegal."

When White privileged people do not risk going into another's cultural domain, we feed the power our dominator culture uses against others. We cannot challenge the narrative our dominant system teaches us without first investigating alternative perspectives and ways of being. And alternative perspectives are best investigated from within the alternative's space.

Through her courageous struggle to be heard and known, Anzaldúa encourages us to be brave as well. "Ignorance splits people, creates prejudices," she writes. "At some point, on our way to a new consciousness, we will have to leave the opposite bank . . . cross the border into a wholly new and separate territory."[11]

Older and heavyset, Juan Pérez wears a back brace and walks painfully slowly. He meets me at the front gate after I have signed in, turned over my driver's license, described the make of my car in the parking lot outside, and received my visitor's badge. The weight of the badge, clipped to my collar, keeps pulling my shirt open at the neck. My hands obsessively search the satin pockets of my coat for the cell phone I had to leave in the car. The worn metal of every door handle makes me wish I'd brought hand sanitizer. After clearing the metal detector, Juan and I are buzzed into the next building. A heavy, motorized door opens slowly in front of us, and we enter a short hallway where our IDs will be checked again. The hallway stretches along a windowed room full of neatly stacked shotguns and hundreds of handcuffs hanging on pegs. The door closes behind us and locks with a loud clang.

Gesturing toward the room with the bulletproof windows, Juan explains, "This is where the weapons are kept."

It unnerves me to be so close to all that firepower.

The door on the opposite side of the hallway unlocks and opens slowly to let us through. As he escorts me through to the prison yard, a block of old, stooped men—all Black and Brown, gray speckling their hair—are halted by a young uniformed guard in black sunglasses so Juan can walk me safely past. I am embarrassed that my visit has impeded their unit's walk to their cell block, embarrassed to be protected from these men who look so old and harmless. I try not to stare. Did I expect all the men in here to be young, virile, and tatted up like a bunch of Hollywood gangbangers?

A chipmunk pops out of a hole by the sidewalk. I smile as he side-eyes the waiting men. Noticing my attention, Juan says, "They feed them."

"What? The chipmunks?" I look back at the men.

"Yes," Juan says as we watch the tiny critter dance and jump as if performing for a treat. Juan's slow pace gives me time to consider the chipmunk. The chipmunk considers me too. I imagine him wondering how I'd made it in here. Did I have to burrow into this yard through elaborately dug tunnels? Did I come for the treats—bread crumbs and peanuts scuttled from the dining hall?

I smile at the chipmunk. Maybe Juan is not the only minister here.

The men wear light-blue prison-issue shirts, navy pants, and white or black tennis shoes. Some have added long-sleeve, white thermal shirts underneath and navy stocking caps for warmth. Later I learn from the thirty-five-page volunteer manual, "Do not wear blue." The snipers perched in the towers surrounding the prison must be able to clearly distinguish me from the men. "Wear comfortable shoes." In case I need to run.

We tour the vocational building, including the chapel—a large, empty room with dirty beige carpet and locked storage closets. Juan pauses inside the door to explain, "This chapel has to serve everyone, all the religions. We pull stuff out for each service, then we put it back."

The classrooms in the vocational building are full of mismatched school desks. One room has multiple rows of new Dell computers, sitting dead along the walls. "We can't use them," Juan says, nodding at the black monitors. "They were bought for a grant program, and the program ended. We're just waiting for them to be picked up." The incarcerated men, I learn, do not have access to the internet.

Juan has been the chaplain here for eighteen years, but his office furniture looks like it arrived already used. He invites me to sit in an old tweed-covered armchair that looks like it was pulled out of someone's living room in the 1970s. I sink low in its broken-down cushion.

An older incarcerated man enters hesitantly and places a guitar case on Juan's desk. "This is Rafael. He's my assistant. Rafael, this is Reverend Ott." Rafael nods politely but seems too spooked by me to speak. Juan opens the case. "Everything must be inspected, before and after use," he explains before handing the instrument back to Rafael. I imagine stolen guitar strings against an incarcerated man's neck as Rafael leaves the office quickly. Relieved, it seems, to escape.

Juan never expected to be a chaplain in corrections. It was a job, though, and they really needed someone. Tears well in his eyes as he speaks about the men he serves and the call he now feels to the incarcerated. But he is also drowning in paperwork. He manages all the volunteers and coordinates background checks.

The phone rings. Someone needs to know where a prisoner is. Juan doesn't have an answer but promises to find out. As we wrap up, Juan pauses to tell me he is glad I came. "I'm retiring in a year. I'd like to get some programs going for these men before I do."

Before making this visit, I'd written a blog post about what led me here and posted it on social media. Faculty friends left comments:

"That prison has been calling to me too. Let me know what you find out."

"Can I go with you next time?"

"Let me know what you learn. I'd like to do something too."

Their comments gave me courage. I wasn't alone.

"Maybe I can help," I say to Juan as we start the arduous walk back to the front gate.

Before we pass back through the arsenal, Juan pauses in front of a small room where a young, incarcerated Latino is meeting with a man and woman in business suits. The Latino man waves excitedly to get Juan's attention. He pokes his head in the door, greets the young man, and asks, "How's every-thing going?"

The inmate nods positively. "It's going great, Chap! It's going great!"

"Bless you. Tell me more later," Juan says as he shuts the door and turns to me. "He's been taken on by the Innocence Project. Those are their lawyers. It's looking really good for him. He'll get out soon."

My breath catches. "Oh my gosh. That's amazing, Juan."

"Yes," he responds with a big smile, "yes, it is."

Goose bumps rise on my skin and tears well up as I con-sider that excited young man—that excited, *innocent* young man—being released. How wonderful yet how tragic. How could he be in this place and be innocent?

Anzaldúa compares the crossing of borders to a dry birth, a screaming, painful birth that fights you every inch of the way. I felt this pain as I crossed through every heavy metal door of the prison. Every step of my tour, I learned something new about Parker Correctional—the staff, the human beings incarcerated inside, the injustices of our justice system. Once I crossed over, I couldn't unlearn what I now knew. I couldn't continue to ignore my community's prison—*ignore*, W. E. B. Du Bois prophetically reminds us, being the root word of *ignorance*.

Anzaldúa writes that "every increment of conscious-ness, every step forward is a *travesia*, a crossing. I am again an alien in a new territory. And again, and again. But if I escape conscious awareness, escape 'knowing,' I won't be moving. Knowledge makes me more aware, it makes me more concil-iatory. 'Knowing' is painful because after 'it' happens I can't stay in the same place and be comfortable. I am no longer the same person I was before."[12]

Juan and I say goodbye at the gate, and I thank him for his time. He starts to shake my hand, then changes his mind and leans in for a hug. I hug him back, grateful for the warmth of touch after such an emotional visit. I sign out, turn in my vis-itor's badge, and get my driver's license back. An incarcerated man is being moved out of the gate—transported to either a trial or another prison. I stand back so the two officers escorting him have enough space. The man's wrists are cuffed and shackled to the front of his waist with a thick chain. I watch as they load him into the back seat of an unmarked white minivan.

The bright sun and expansive midwestern sky give me pause once I am outside. I enjoy a gust of spring wind before climbing into my car and grabbing my cell phone to check for missed calls and emails. I remember Chris Hoke's challenge to the church: go to prison, meet the incarcerated, learn about their lives, consider their conditions, and experience their humanity. Now that I had taken this step on my own, I understood why he believed this would change us.

I start the fifteen-minute drive back to my college. DO NOT PICK UP HITCHHIKERS, the sign on the highway warns—too late. I can see their faces and hear their voices. The prison isn't just a slab of cement surrounded by a chain-link fence. It's the place where Juan, and Rafael, and the young man wrongly accused spend their days. I want to go back. I want to learn more. I want to violate all that keeps us apart.

When White privileged people do not risk going, we send the message that we do not care to know, or worse, that we believe we are better—and better off separate. What keeps us from crossing borders—our fear, our prejudice, our ignorance—can and should be overcome. I've learned this in a profound way at the prison, returning as often as I can to volunteer teach. I feared the incarcerated men based on racial prejudice and stereotypes. I also feared their rejection when I first taught there. I expected them to react negatively to me. Like, who's this crazy White woman coming in here thinking she can teach us? Instead, I was wholeheartedly welcomed. These men are so hungry to be known. They feel forgotten by society. They hunger for their humanity to be recognized and honored by people on the outside.

I've felt something similar from the college students of color when I've risked reaching out to them. I was not dismissed as an out-of-touch, privileged White lady, as I feared I would be. Rather, my attention and my desire to connect were welcomed and appreciated. No one wants to be ignored. Everyone wants to be known.

But we White privileged people need to practice careful listening in order to discern which spaces we should risk entering. When racial tension ran high on my college campus, administrators called a town hall gathering for students, faculty, and staff to speak and be heard. The students of color repeatedly stood up to share a common complaint: "We host programs, and you don't come." Some of the White students responded, "But I didn't know I could come. I didn't think those programs were for me." In other words, they failed to hear these public programs as invitations to risk going. They had too quickly scrolled past or ignored the emails publicly welcoming them. By listening even more carefully, these students could have discerned where they were *not* being invited—to the small groups or club meetings these students of color claim as their own, spaces where they can relax as themselves and be around others who understand their experience without much explanation or the tiring need to teach.

When I stopped to consider whether I should risk going to the prison, I had to know to whom the space belonged. It quickly became clear that the incarcerated men did not view the prison as "their" space. Welcome to the "gray waste," the incarcerated men would say, referring to the prison where few risk going unless they have to. I also learned that corrections is designed to control and strip the incarcerated of their humanity. When "outsiders" risk going to prison and risk getting to know the incarcerated, we can help rehumanize people in a cold, controlling system.

But even if a space is "theirs," listen for an invitation. I have occasionally visited a predominantly Black worship service and been warmly welcomed, since the culture of this church is rooted in hospitality. Before accepting an invitation, though, take some time to do your research—read some articles, watch some YouTube videos—and learn how to be a good guest. What are the customs, rituals, expectations of the community you are visiting? Reduce the risk of making mistakes by doing your homework first.

Crossing borders is painful but necessary. On the other side, we see things from a different perspective, and abstract "others" become human beings whom we once ignored and objectivized. To be in solidarity with those who are oppressed, we must honor their humanity by leaving our comfortable spaces of privilege and respectfully, carefully enter their space— not to "fix them" or to "help them" meet the standards of our

White culture but to meet them and know them for who they are and where they are.

"We ask to be met halfway," writes Anzaldúa. "This is your invitation."[13]

Suggested Action Steps to Risk Going

1. "Get proximate to suffering and injustice," as Bryan Stevenson suggests. Think of places in your community where you can volunteer to experience the humanity of those who suffer, places where issues such as incarceration, poverty, homelessness, and hunger become less abstract and more personal—your local prison, soup kitchen, community home, homeless or domestic violence shelter, or after-school program.

2. Partner with other community groups. Encourage your faith community to reach out to and partner with another community that is predominantly non-White or of a different religion. Read and discuss together a book such as *Borderlands* or Martin Luther King Jr.'s *Where Do We Go from Here: Chaos or Community?* Or partner on a joint service project where members of each community can get to know one another by working side by side.

3. Attend public events. Watch for announcements and invitations to public events in your community hosted by groups of other races or religions—festivals, fundraisers, worship services, concerts, and performances. Invite friends or other church members to go with you and afterward discuss what you learned and observed.

Chapter Two

Risk Staying

Guilt and defensiveness are bricks in a wall against
which we all flounder; they serve none of our futures.

—AUDRE LORDE, *Sister Outsider*

By the fall of 2017, my weekly religious life program had
grown to include a large group of Latinx students. In
September of that year, US Attorney General Jeff Sessions
announced that the DACA program established under President Barack Obama would be rescinded. Students affected by
this announcement were hurt and afraid. Adding to their pain
was the lack of knowledge about DACA among their White
peers. So I decided to dedicate my weekly program to the topic.
We discussed DACA and Sessions's argument that Obama's executive action was an unconstitutional exercise of authority by
the executive branch because it circumvented the legislative

process. We shared information about the need DACA was meant to address, who it affected, and how we could respond to Sessions's announcement by writing letters to our legislators. Then I invited the students to share, saying, "OK, now we're going to have a time of listening. I know this has been really hard for some of you. Feel free to share whatever you are thinking or feeling."

We held our program in two adjoining living rooms of our college's Presbyterian House. That evening, about thirty-five students showed up. I sat on a folding chair at one end of the adjoining rooms, while the students sat on the floor or scattered along the walls on couches and chairs. As I broached this "time of listening," I was eager to do right for our students of color. Dontae, an outspoken African American student who was passionate about justice, sat partially hidden behind the pocket door that separated the two rooms. It bothered me that I could hear her voice but couldn't see her face. Keeara, attending for the first time, stood to my left like an uneasy sentinel, hovering in the doorway leading to the dining room. She participated in the discussion but never sat down. Jocelyn, one of my student interns, sat on a couch to my right with two other Latina students. Andrea, another Latina intern, sat in the back of the far living room in my direct line of sight. I focused on her thoughtful, kind face as I led the discussion.

Dontae and Keeara were critical of our college's response to the news about DACA. Why did the college do this? Why didn't the college do that? Although I was not part of our college's senior administration, I heard a critique of myself and my leadership in their questions. So I shared what I knew from the college's perspective and defended our administrators against comments that I felt were unfair. My words were met, though, with silence, and the room grew tense. I couldn't figure out why this was happening or where I had gone wrong, so I just kept talking, affirming our students for their thoughts while also trying to help them understand the college administration's perspective. Nothing I said improved the mood in the room.

After the program, I pulled Andrea aside to ask her if she thought the evening went OK. What I really needed to know, though, was if I was OK. Did I mess up? Did I come off wrong? Did I say something I shouldn't have said? My insecurity was running on overdrive.

Andrea confirmed what I already knew. In my attempt to be fair to the administration and present their perspective, I had come off as defensive to students who, feeling betrayed by their country and their community, needed a place to talk—and needed the White leader in the room to simply listen, affirm their feelings, and acknowledge their pain.

I walked away from that program feeling like a failure, unable to revisit the conversation, not just because the students had scattered but because I'd had enough for one day. I embraced the "out" my privilege grants and retreated home to lick my wounds and talk to my husband, who has always loved me through my mistakes.

It took me a few years to gain enough distance on this situation to examine it and learn from it. Now that I have, I've committed to keep placing myself in these uncomfortable situations. How I felt during that program—trying to find the right words, trying to express myself, my opinions, and my perspective without offending the students of color—was excruciating. But Jocelyn and Andrea feel this way every day as they seek to express themselves at a White institution within a dominant White culture. They never have the choice to be uncomfortable or not. Why, then, should I?

Although she has been critiqued for infantilizing Black people,[1] reading Robin DiAngelo's *White Fragility* was another turning point in my continual journey out of privileged ignorance. DiAngelo was the first to help me understand how I and other White people habitually, instinctively withdraw from uncomfortable conversations about race with a range of defensive responses—anger, fear, argumentation, silence, or tears. As I expanded my sources, I discovered Resmaa Menakem, who cites DiAngelo but goes further in explaining how these "fragile" responses are trauma-driven, fight, flee, or freeze responses to the embodied myth that White people are vulnerable and in need of protection from Black people. This myth of fragility serves us well, protecting us and our White systems from challenge, justifying White violence as self-defense.

In particular, DiAngelo's chapter "White Women's Tears" made me realize why I had to find a way to be less fragile in conversations about race and privilege. Racial justice educators will often begin workshops by telling White participants that they should take a break and leave the room if they feel moved to tears or feel their emotions getting out of control. This ground rule—no White tears in conversations about race—has been celebrated by Black people while infuriating to White people. The rule can feel counterintuitive to White people, especially women, who often value showing emotion as a way of reflecting compassion and support. On the surface, it can also feel unfair. In a conversation where Black people vulnerably share deep frustrations and anger, White people wonder, "Why do *they* get to show emotion but *we* can't?" Here, DiAngelo points us to the historical and political implications of White women's tears. Emmett Till was beaten, tortured, and murdered because a White woman claimed the fourteen-year-old had flirted with her. The woman recanted her story later, admitting she had lied. Till's mother demanded an open casket at Emmett's funeral; she demanded the world view his mutilated body to reckon with his tragic death and the brutal consequences of our racism. Countless Black men have lost their lives to protect the fragile White woman in distress. This traumatizing history gets triggered and played out in today's conversations on race.

Whites must also recognize how our emotional reactions—whether they surface as tears, angry defensiveness, or knee-jerk excuses and denials—deflect the focus from the important conversation at hand and toward the upset White person. In an article for *Everyday Feminism*, Jennifer Loubriel writes about why she is a big fan of the "no white tears" rule: "Rather than focusing on the lived experiences and traumas of People of Color . . . or how [we] feel on an everyday basis from having to deal with racist institutions, interpersonal relationships, and ideologies, the focus goes to white people just beginning to confront how they benefit from racism on many levels."[2]

I've felt the painful stab of shame and guilt so many times in conversations related to race, I can't recollect them all. Like the time I enthusiastically told a Black student how "he spoke so eloquently," as if I'd never heard a Black person speak intelligently before. *Ugh.* My husband was present and called me out on that one. Or when I read a Black person's tweet angrily condemning White writers who do not capitalize "Black." *Damn.* I've done that so often. *But I didn't know! How am I supposed to always know what the correct term is or the correct use?* And there I go again, getting defensive.

In the face of an angry Black person's words, particularly if I hear myself in the charge they are making, I crumble inside. Black anger makes me afraid to speak up, join conversations about race and diversity, or ask questions. I'm convinced my questions will be stupid and just further marginalize an already marginalized person by making them bear the responsibility for my education. Being a White privileged person trying to talk about race feels like walking on eggshells. I'd much rather go crawl into a hole.

But if I avoid, or deflect, or get defensive, or seek refuge from the difficulty of the conversation or the pain of accusation, I will not be a part of the process of change. More significantly, I will be a part of the problem. "Guilt and defensiveness are bricks in a wall against which we all flounder," writes Audre Lorde. "They serve none of our futures."[3] I must risk staying in the moment when my knee-jerk attempt to defend the status quo is challenged, or when an email I send is critiqued as biased, or when my leadership is questioned by students demanding more systemic change. Even when staying feels like bathing in buckets of shame.

Brené Brown's research on shame is helpful here. "Shame," Brown writes, "is the fear of disconnection. We are psychologically, emotionally, cognitively, and spiritually hardwired for connection, love, and belonging. . . . Shame is the fear that something we've done or failed to do, an ideal that we've not lived up to, or a goal that we've not accomplished makes us unworthy of connection. I'm unlovable. I don't belong." Unlike guilt, which focuses on something we *did* wrong, shame focuses on our *being* wrong. And the pain of this emotion is real. Brown writes, "Researchers [have] found that, as far as the brain is concerned, physical pain and intense experiences of social rejection hurt in the same way."[4]

When it comes to race relations, White people should be appropriately ashamed. There's no weaseling our way out of the historic, systematic oppression White people have inflicted on others. Acknowledging and accepting this truth as well as the ways I have benefited as a White person from systems and structures that oppress others has helped me find the courage to stay in some uncomfortable conversations and situations.

Shame resilience, according to Brown, is the ability to be vulnerable, connected, and fully engaged without condemning ourselves as bad, unworthy, or flawed when we make mistakes. Developing this ability will help us risk staying in important conversations with people of color. "Shame erodes our courage and fuels disengagement,"[5] two crucial components for successful dialogue on difficult subjects. Therefore, we must recognize shame when it rises within us and name it as the enemy of our efforts to listen, connect, and learn.

As a pastor, I've experienced the liberating power of confession for others and for myself. Burying our shame, or keeping it secret, only stokes its flame. As soon as we name our wrongs and share them with a trusted person, shame loses much of its heat. This is why twelve-step programs begin with participants naming themselves as addicts.

Recently, I audited a poetry class. There was only one other student older than forty in the class, which felt awkward to me. But the job perk of free college classes outweighed this slight discomfort. Our class reflected our college in that it was predominantly White; the only person of color appeared to be the other older student, who was an Indian woman.

One day our White professor led us in a discussion of Eve Ewing's book of poetry, *1919*, based on the Chicago race riot of 1919. The book's poetry includes excerpts of a fascinating report of the riot discovered by the poet in her research. In 1922 the governor asked a special committee of six Black men and six White men to study the riot and provide recommendations so such a tragedy would never reoccur. I had no idea racial justice efforts like this took place in 1922. As our discussion of the book wound down, our professor asked, "Could I, as a White person, write a book like this? Off this history?"

I appreciated the question. A controversy over the publication and promotion of *American Dirt* by Jeanine Cummins had recently filled my social media feeds, especially among my writer friends. The novel tells the story of Mexicans migrating to the United States, but the author was not Mexican and was accused of exacerbating harmful stereotypes. Published by a division of Macmillan (one of the top five publishing powerhouses), this White author's book was supported with a lot of money for marketing and promoting. In response, lists of alternative books to buy and read about immigration written by Latinx authors were curated and shared widely on the internet.

One student responded quickly to our professor's question: "No, *you* couldn't write this book."

I raised my hand. A simple no didn't feel right. The professor's question was more complex. "Doesn't all history belong to all of us?"

A rising sound of "Mmmmmm!" cut me short. A girl on the other side of the room was calling me out for what I'd just said.

"Now, wait," I asserted, my palm up to stop her accusation. I hadn't even finished my thought! "We can all write from history when we locate ourselves in that history and write from that location."

The professor nodded. "Yes." Then he suggested, "So maybe the history doesn't belong to us, but we belong to the history, and we write from that?"

I nodded, but I'd also caught his correction. My statement about history *belonging* to all of us insinuated a White racial habit of possessiveness and appropriation—taking other people, cultures, histories as our own.

Shannon Sullivan also writes about the White habit of commodifying everything[6]—transforming people, culture, history into objects we can own or possess. If history belongs to us, it serves as our objective possession to do with as we see fit. For example, White people have long been accused of whitewashing history by softening our abuses and avoiding, distorting, or lying about the truth of our oppression and enslavement of others. But if we belong to history, history possesses itself. It stands alone and cannot be manipulated by those who have the most power.

My choice of words embarrassed me—especially as an adult, the chaplain no less, in a room full of college kids. Shame flamed hot within me and spread so quickly, I couldn't think anymore, distracted by messages of my unworthiness. *You're so stupid. You know better. How could you let yourself get schooled by a twenty-year-old, purple-haired, poet girl who can't even show up for class half the time?*

I tried my best to recover enough in class to rejoin the discussion. I was proud of myself for at least not letting her interruption stop me from getting my whole thought out. When I was a shy college student struggling to find her voice, I never would have had the courage to continue after being cut off. In uncomfortable moments such as these, however, it's also important to recognize that sometimes our feelings are disproportionate to the situation. The best advice I received as a pastor of a congregation was from Barbara Brown Taylor's book *Leaving Church*: "The people you think love you don't love you as much as you think they love you, and the people you think hate you don't hate you as much as you think they hate you."[7]

Nevertheless, I couldn't let go of the shame of being corrected, perhaps especially by a White student. After reflecting on this situation, I recognize that I am much more willing to be corrected by people of color on issues of race, regardless of their age, because I trust that they are speaking from experience. But I've also come to understand that White people must confront other White people so that the burden of racial justice work does not all fall on people of color. This correction may have stung more because of who delivered it and how it was shared, but my choice of words was misguided.

Immediately after our class was dismissed, I called my husband. Dan is the person I most often trust to receive my confessions. I know he will receive my mistakes with empathy and still love me afterward.

"Listen to this. Listen to what I did this time. I feel horrible." Dan listened and commiserated. After naming my shame and receiving Dan's grace and empathy, I felt like I'd been released from a great weight. Years ago, in a shame situation like this, I would have responded by withdrawing, going silent, or dropping the class altogether. (I mean, I was taking it only for my own edification.) But I don't want to be that person anymore. My values and my faith call me to courage, not fragility. So I returned to the poetry class, determined to learn from my mistakes and keep raising my hand.

Brown writes, "Shame resilience is the ability to say, 'This hurts. This is disappointing, maybe even devastating. But success and recognition and approval are not the values that drive me. My value is courage and I was just courageous. You can move on, shame.'"[8]

45

❉

When considering how to develop resilience as a person of privilege, it's also important to put our feelings of shame in perspective. Ibram X. Kendi's work mapping our nation's history of racist ideas reveals the shame messages Black people have had to endure since they were forcibly brought to our shores. The title of Kendi's book, *Stamped from the Beginning: The Definitive History of Racist Ideas in America*, comes from a speech given by Mississippi senator Jefferson Davis on April 12, 1860, stating that the "inequality of the white and black races" was "stamped from the beginning." The racist ideas that Black people are biologically, culturally, and behaviorally inferior to White people have shaped our nation's history, our political policies, our societal systems and structures. Kendi's important book traces the history of these ideas from their origins in fifteenth-century Europe to support the trade of chattel slaves, through colonial times when the British settlers carried racist ideas to America, all the way to the twenty-first century and current debates about the killing of Black people by police and the Black Lives Matter movement.[9]

Internalizing such painful racist ideas and shame messages such as *You are not worthy*, *You are inferior*, and *You are less than human* has traumatized and inhibited Black people for generations. Before long, a person hearing such messages starts believing they are true. "Self-depreciation is a characteristic of the oppressed," writes Paulo Friere. "So often do they hear that they are good for nothing, know nothing and are incapable of learning anything—that they are sick, lazy, and unproductive—that in the end they become convinced of their own unfitness."[10]

Overcoming such traumatizing forces depends on what Freire describes as the *conscientização* of society, the development of a critical awareness by oppressed and oppressor alike of how society has been structured on such racist ideas. The oppressed develop shame resilience by rejecting the racist ideas of the oppressor and believing in themselves. "It is only when the oppressed find the oppressor out," Friere writes, "and become involved in the organized struggle for their liberation that they begin to believe in themselves."[11]

Jocelyn was referred to me for counseling in her first year at our college. She was smart and capable but was going home every weekend and thinking of dropping out. We'd meet occasionally to talk and pray. During one conversation, not knowing the impact it would have, I asked Jocelyn if she had ever heard of the book *Mujerista Theology* by Ada María Isasi-Díaz. *Mujer* means "woman" in Spanish, and mujerista theology is a Hispanic feminist liberation theology, developed out of Isasi-Díaz's experiences as a Cuban-born Latina scholar living in the United States. For her, the feminist movement of the 1970s and 1980s was preoccupied with the experience of White Anglo women. She saw the need for a theological method that took seriously the religious understandings and practices of Latina women. Mujerista theology is more than a doctrine, more than a theory. It is itself a liberative praxis, a reflective action that empowers Latinas to be theologians themselves.

Jocelyn had never heard of it and quickly got a copy of the book. When next we met, she held *Mujerista Theology* out in front of her. "I love this picture."

I hadn't paid attention to the image on the cover, a large Latina cook cupping a clay pot, until Jocelyn pointed it out. "You know," I responded, "I haven't even read the whole book myself. I only read excerpts in seminary. Would you like to read it together?"

"Yes!" Jocelyn's eyes lit up. "I'd love that."

"Great. We can read it over summer break and message each other about it or talk by phone."

I felt slightly selfish in this invitation, thinking I might get more out of reading *Mujerista Theology* with a young Latina than Jocelyn would get from reading it with me. But we were both enthusiastic.

When I messaged Jocelyn on Facebook about our reading, she messaged back saying she had been on the phone with her best friend and roommate, Andrea (another Latina student), reading *Mujerista Theology* aloud. *Teri*, she wrote, *this book is rocking my world. It's gold. Pure gold.*

When we met later, Jocelyn helped me understand the impact of Isasi-Díaz's work. "When I first started reading," Jocelyn said, "I was confused how this woman knew what I was thinking. It was hard to keep reading because I had to stop every few minutes and reread—I just couldn't believe it. Isasi-Díaz dives into ideas or thoughts that we know as Latinas."

"It's back here," Jocelyn described, waving her hands behind her head, "but we can't bring it to the forefront. We can't put it into words. She does that for us."

As Jocelyn shared, I began to better understand Isasi-Díaz and recalled this passage from her book:

> *La vida es la lucha*—the struggle is life. For over half my life I thought my task was to struggle and then one day I would enjoy the fruits of my labor. This is the kind of resignation and expectation of being rewarded in the next life that the Roman Catholic Church has taught for centuries. Then I began to reflect on what my mother often tells the family: "All we need to ask of God is to have health and strength to struggle. As long as we have what we need to struggle in life, we need ask for nothing else." This understanding gives me much strength in my everyday life. It has allowed me to be realistic—to understand that, for the vast majority of women, life is an ongoing struggle. But above all it has made me realize that I can and should relish the struggle. The struggle is my life.[12]

Jocelyn couldn't stop smiling as she spoke about the book. Isasi-Díaz was helping her articulate why she felt out of place at our predominantly White college with White norms and White expectations. Isasi-Díaz also helped Jocelyn understand herself in a way that did not discount or degrade her as "the different one" but empowered her as a Latina woman with unique gifts and perspectives to share. Mujerista theology was what she needed to develop her shame resilience, reject the racist ideas of the oppressor, and believe in herself.

Audre Lorde has served Black people in this way, particularly Black women seeking to reject racist and misogynistic ideas. In her essay "Uses of the Erotic: The Erotic as Power," Lorde writes, "We have been raised to fear the *yes* within ourselves."[13] Lorde's use of the word *erotic* in this essay comes from the Greek word *eros*, which she defines as "the personification of love in all its aspects—born of Chaos, and personifying creative power and harmony."[14] Lorde describes how the erotic empowers her in the face of debilitating and dehumanizing messages. "In touch with the erotic," she writes, "I become less willing to accept powerlessness, or those other supplied states of being which are not native to me, such as resignation, despair, self-effacement, depression, self-denial."[15]

Given the resilience people of color must develop to survive, White people need to understand why our fragility in conversations about race is so detrimental. "Shame," Brown writes, "kills creativity and innovation. It keeps us small, resentful and afraid."[16] Just think of all we could accomplish if we White privileged people developed our own shame resilience. Think of all the injustices we could help make right if we could move beyond our fear of making mistakes, of vulnerability, of change, of full engagement with people who are different from us. "All too often guilt [and shame are] just another name for impotence," Lorde writes. It destroys any chance for productive conversation. "It becomes a device to protect ignorance and the continuation of things the way they are, the ultimate protection for changelessness."[17]

It's not our mistakes or missteps that define us but the values we hold and live by. Let us ask ourselves, Is our behavior guided more by our fear of making mistakes and the consequences of those mistakes or by the courage we value and seek to live by? Are our actions inspired by a call to equity and inclusion or our desire to please and avoid uncomfortable change? When White privileged people risk staying in uncomfortable yet necessary conversations about race, we embody the values, courage, and resilience needed to transform unjust societal structures.

Suggested Action Steps to Risk Staying

1. Read this article by Jennifer Loubriel, a queer, mixed-race activist: "4 Ways White People Can Process Their Emotions without Bringing the White Tears" (https://everydayfeminism.com/2016/02/white-people-emotions-tears/). Discuss it with a group of White friends.

2. Share your commitment to risk staying with a few trusted friends, family members, or religious leaders. Ask them if they would be willing to serve as your "priests" to receive your shame confessions with empathy and grace so you can continue to live into your value of courage.

3. Recall and reflect upon the last time you found yourself in an uncomfortable conversation about

race. How did you feel? What did you think?
How did you respond? Write your thoughts and
feelings in a journal. Share the memory of this
scene with a trusted friend, and articulate how
you would like to respond when you find yourself
in a similar situation.

Chapter Three

Risk Learning

We hear it is the task of women of Color to educate
white women as to our existence, our differences, our
relative roles in our joint survival. This is a diversion
of energies and a tragic repetition of racist patriarchal
thought.

—AUDRE LORDE, "The Master's Tools Will
Never Dismantle the Master's House"

D r. Eddie Glaude Jr., professor of religion and African
American studies at Princeton University, visited the
college I served as chaplain to lecture on his book *Democracy in
Black*. When Glaude concluded his lecture, he paused to take
a question from a White female professor. I cringed when the
question turned into a speech, the point of which seemed to
be to inform everyone what a good, enlightened liberal she
was. The speech also included a message for students of color

to share their experiences so others could learn from them. "I tell my students to teach me, to help me learn," this professor concluded passionately, as if everyone should give her a round of applause.

I was annoyed by this woman's speechifying. But I didn't actually see her message as problematic. In fact, I had done the same thing when traveling with a Latina student on a spring break trip. After a deep, meaningful conversation about issues of race in America, I leaned toward her to make what I considered a humble gesture: "You know, I'm going to make mistakes. And I want you to feel free to correct me. I want to learn. I want you to teach me." She didn't say anything in response, her eyes on mine, attentively polite but heavy—a look I couldn't interpret.

Glaude listened thoughtfully to the self-congratulatory professor and paused. Then he said, "You know, it's *tiring* trying to teach people all the time. There are books you can read." And the Black and Latinx students in the room exploded in spontaneous, raucous applause.

The moment left me reeling. I suddenly understood the burden I had placed on that young Latina student. Expecting her to correct me. Expecting her to teach me. How could I have not seen the position that put her in? How could I not have seen how awkward that must have felt, to have the teacher (or the chaplain, in my case) ask the student to take responsibility for the teacher's own education?

I remembered this experience again while reading Audre Lorde. Addressing White women in her essay "The Master's Tools Will Never Dismantle the Master's House," Lorde writes, "Women of today are still being called upon to stretch across the gap of male ignorance and to educate men as to our existence and needs. This is an old and primary tool of all oppressors to keep the oppressed occupied with the master's concerns. Now, we hear it is the task of women of Color to educate white women as to our existence, our differences, our relative roles in our joint survival. This is a diversion of energies and a tragic repetition of racist patriarchal thought."[1]

Privileged people perpetuate injustice when we fail to take responsibility for our own education. When we burden those who are less privileged with the task of teaching us, we divert their precious limited energy from resisting daily oppression. But because our privilege blinds and protects us from systemic, societal injustices, it's difficult to know where and how to begin learning.

Dr. Eddie Glaude's simple yet profound challenge was what finally got me started.

There are books we can read. Lots of them, in fact. I cite many authors from whom I have learned and have included a resource list at the back of this book for further reading. But I started by reading a few of the newly popular books by White racial justice educators such as Debby Irving, Jennifer Harvey, and Robin DiAngelo. It was important for me to begin by reading White authors on racial justice because I needed my eyes opened to the fact that "White" is a socially constructed race all its own. When we swim in a White world, we need to learn to see the water.

Debby Irving's memoir, *Waking Up White, and Finding Myself in the Story of Race*, resonated with me because her White suburban upbringing closely matched my own. Her questions and struggles resonated as well. Before her racial awakening, Irving writes, "If someone had called me a racist, I would have kicked and screamed in protest. 'But I'm a good person! I don't see color!'" Later she begins to question the "culture of niceness" in which she was raised, realizing that this expectation of "niceness" best serves those for whom life is going well and those in power. Irving writes, "The culture of niceness provides a tidy cover, creating a social norm that says conflict is bad, discomfort should be avoided, and those who create them mark themselves as people who lack the kind of emotional restraint necessary to hold positions of power."[2]

Irving's naming of such White cultural traits was eye opening for me. I was fortunate to attend a workshop she led where she shared other characteristics of our dominant White culture, such as valuing self-sufficiency, believing formal education is the best education, and viewing time as a scarce commodity. For me, understanding these characteristics as derived from my White culture was hugely significant. Suddenly I realized that my White ways of living and being and believing are not universal. Other cultures have other values, and mine are not necessarily the best. Yet when my culture is the dominant culture, all others must adjust to my White standards and expectations.

Jennifer Harvey's book *Raising White Kids: Bringing Up Children in a Racially Unjust America* is not just for parents of White children. Harvey hopes to move us beyond the "color-blind" teaching of the past toward what she calls "race-conscious" parenting. Harvey believes race-conscious parenting will deepen our active commitment to everyone's children by drawing more of us into the larger movement of social and racial justice—a movement that Harvey says needs "all of us to be *all in*." Yet in order for us to be "all in," we White people need to better equip ourselves for conversations about race and racism.

Harvey's book led me to better understand my White students who go silent whenever the topic of race arises. I had interpreted this silence as a lack of courage or a lack of interest. My White students would just sit there with blank looks on their faces while all the students of color spoke and shared. The blank faces frustrated and angered me. "Why don't you care?" I wanted to shout at them. Harvey, who teaches at Drake University, offered me a more empathetic perspective. She describes how her White students struggle to find a meaningful place from which to participate fully in conversations about diversity and race, even while they get pressure from adults to do so as they grow older. Her White students are often aware that racial tensions exist. Many of them also know or sense that these tensions have to do with injustices White people have committed. But since they (unlike students of color) have not been actively nurtured in their understanding of race and its meaning in their lives, they are ill-equipped to participate in conversations when the topic arises. Young people need to grow up with nuanced, supportive, and complex discussions about race, says Harvey, in order to engage positively and meaningfully in diverse, multicultural settings.

After I had read a few books by White racial justice educators, I recognized my need to decenter White voices and

White scholarship in my learning. I needed to move on to primary sources, to the books of seminal thought leaders of color whose work first inspired the racial justice education of today. Martin Luther King Jr., James Baldwin, Audre Lorde, bell hooks, Gloria Anzaldúa, and many others have helped me grow in awareness and understanding by reflecting on my White life and how my life—my actions, inactions, conscious and subconscious beliefs, and behaviors—affects those with less privilege than me.

I started with James Baldwin's *Notes of a Native Son*, which I had always meant to read but never made a priority. I was thoroughly enjoying myself, getting to know Baldwin's work, until I came to a scene that brought me to an abrupt stop. In this scene, set in 1950 in New York City, Baldwin describes the rage, the blind fever that finally overcame him after he was repeatedly turned away from being served at restaurants and diners because of the color of his skin. In one such restaurant, a young White waitress with "great, astounded, frightened eyes" was sent to tell the hungry Baldwin that he would not be fed. Baldwin writes,

> [The waitress] did not ask me what I wanted, but repeated, as though she had learned it somewhere, "We don't serve Negroes here." She did not say it with the blunt, derisive hostility to which I had grown so accustomed, but, rather, with a note of apology in her voice, and fear. This made me colder and more murderous than ever. Somehow, with the repetition of that phrase, which was already ringing in my

head like a thousand bells of a nightmare, I realized she would never come any closer and that I would have to strike from a distance. There was nothing on the table but an ordinary water-mug half full of water, and I picked this up and hurled it with all my strength at her.[3]

Baldwin's violent rage upended me. At first, I did not want to understand, because to understand the rage made it acceptable—and it was too frightening to be acceptable, too violent for any justification. I fought with myself, tempted to close the book. How easy it would be to dismiss Baldwin as just another dangerous Black man.

I couldn't close the book, though, because I found myself in Baldwin's story. The White waitress was not me, but she could have been. She followed the norms and rules set by White society. She did as her employers told her to do. She was sorry for what she knew was wrong but not sorry enough to change, or rebel, or even push against the racist status quo. The dark stranger seated at her table in the restaurant was frightening. But she was more afraid of what she risked losing as a good White woman—her job, her reputation, her position of privilege—than she was of the raging Black man. She felt powerless, even though she wasn't. She had a voice, but she used it only to perpetuate her own domination. She had a body, but no muscle of hers moved to cross the line of segregation or privilege. She didn't act, she didn't rebel, she didn't speak up or out because she knew that the angry Black man had more to fear from the restaurant full of White people and the White owners and the White police officers who would come when *she* called. She was safe to do nothing. So even though she empathized with the Black man's plight, all she offered Baldwin was a note—a tone—of apology as she rejected him like everyone else.

Later, Baldwin came to terms with his anger, noting the destructive nature of hatred, which, he said, "never fails to destroy the man who hates." But he also wrote that there is not a Black person alive "who does not have this rage in his blood."[4] And although they are more restrained, I recalled hearing this rage simmering in the voices of my students like Denton and Jocelyn, Dontae and Andrea, who are frustrated and tired, angry and resentful that White privileged people today still fail to understand.

Once I started reading, the risk of learning became evident. Guilt and shame were my constant companions as I awakened from my dream state of privilege, the White fog that had protected me from knowing how I had benefited from the oppression of others. But as I read, I also found inspiration and encouragement, wondering to myself why I hadn't made this learning a priority sooner.

Privileged people have a lot to learn, but we also have a lot to unlearn. We develop racial habits from childhood, learning to value White lives over Black and Brown. The neighborhoods, schools, and churches in which I grew up were all predominantly White. My family moved every few years around the state of Michigan as my father was promoted to higher positions in his bank. Going into my sophomore year of high school, we moved to Bloomfield Hills, Michigan, an affluent suburb of Detroit, which my parents chose for its excellent school. Our house, a two-story colonial at the end of a cul-de-sac, was modest for a neighborhood known for mansions. One of the Detroit Pistons lived nearby in a palatial estate protected by a brick wall and an imposing black iron gate. Other than this NBA player, though, I don't remember having any other people of color as neighbors.

When we grow up without color, anyone who is not White will always appear to be strange, different, and "other." In these White contexts, stereotypes are fed because there is no one nearby to dispel them. Michael Jackson, Whitney Houston, and Jackie Joyner-Kersee were my models of Black life and culture. So, I reasoned, all Black people can dance, are athletic, and have rhythm. When my track team's bus transported us to a predominantly Black school close to Detroit, I was intimidated. I assumed I couldn't win among those athletes.

As much as I admired these stereotypical Black traits— coveted them, even—I also instinctively knew that I did not want to be Black, because being Black, according to news highlighting crime in African American communities, also meant being poor and dangerous. When my family ventured into the city of Detroit for special events, I carefully guarded my purse and felt my body respond to Black males by going rigid and tense.

In her book *Revealing Whiteness: The Unconscious Habits of Racial Privilege*, philosopher Shannon Sullivan credits W. E. B. Du Bois with the idea of unconscious racist habits. Based on his study of William James and Sigmund Freud, Du Bois recognized that any fight against racism would be thwarted if it did not acknowledge and seek to change the unconscious racist habits and "irrational urges" of White people. These racial habits, Sullivan further defines, are not simply our routines, or what we call our "bad habits," like smoking, but rather the way we have been structured (physically, psychologically, socially, politically) as people to interact (Sullivan uses the word *transact*) with the world and the people around us.[5]

Glaude writes in his book *Democracy in Black* about how our racial habits are built into our brain's wiring from an early age. Just like riding a bike, we don't even have to think about our response to Black and Brown people; we simply act or feel out of habit. But racial habits can be changed and transformed by becoming more critically aware of our physical, emotional, and cognitive responses to people of color. This takes constant self-examination and mindful attention to our thoughts and reactions—crucial introspection because, according to Glaude, these racial habits shape not only our personal lives but, even more damaging, the policies and systems we create that reinforce the valuing of White lives over Black and Brown: systems like education, public housing, employment, and criminal justice—systems built by those in the dominant majority and that keep White supremacy alive in America today.

Books can't be our only means of education, though. We also need to risk learning in relationships and conversations with people whose lives and perspectives are different from our own. Unlike people of color who must constantly accommodate to White culture and White dominance in their schools, places of employment, government, and so forth, White privileged people are (for the most part) free to segregate our lives by race.

Years ago, during a pastoral care class I was taking for my doctorate of ministry degree, I was challenged by a fellow student of Middle Eastern descent to reconsider the excuses I used to justify my White surroundings. At the time I served as the pastor of a small church in North Carolina that was 100 percent White. When I shared this fact during a class conversation, the Middle Eastern student, who served as the pastor of a multiethnic church in Chicago, looked startled and then said, with a tone of pity, "Oh, then you do not know what the kingdom of God looks like."

I balked at his words, offended. How could he assume I did not know what the kingdom of God looks like? Sure, my church wasn't diverse, but that didn't mean we weren't good people doing good work. Plus, he clearly didn't understand how hard it was to attract people of color to our church. It's much easier in an urban context like Chicago.

Since then, I've learned enough to recognize that my knee-jerk defensiveness of my White congregation (and my White life) was a self-protective racial habit blinding me to the truth. God's kingdom and God's creation are colorful and diverse. If we live in a White world, we live in a false reality, and we segregate ourselves from the world God has created and desires for us.

My move to campus ministry gave me the chance to serve a more diverse population—an opportunity that excited me. But a few years into my chaplaincy, I noticed that the students attending my programs came from predominantly mainline Protestant backgrounds—Presbyterians like myself, Lutherans, and Methodists. We attracted a few lapsed Catholics looking for something new. The majority were White.

I told myself students of color weren't attending because they didn't know me yet and didn't know that I was an ally. But I hadn't reached out to them. In fact, I felt insecure and awkward around students of color, aware of my White privilege and my ignorance of their reality. I'd smile and say "hello" as I passed them on campus, catching myself being overly friendly. But I wouldn't sit down at the "Black students' table" in the dining hall, telling myself they needed their space and I shouldn't intrude. I wanted to overcome these personal obstacles and find ways to connect, but doing so would lead me into unfamiliar relationship territory. It was easier for me to believe that what I was offering was good enough. If students of color didn't choose to participate, that was OK.

Reading Robin DiAngelo's *White Fragility: Why It's So Hard for White People to Talk about Racism* was pivotal for me. I recognized that I was avoiding situations that might include racial stress or even the potential of racial stress. I also recognized that my White fragility served me as a means of controlling my environment and keeping it safe—meaning predominantly White. If I truly desired a diverse program, the onus was on me to risk reaching out to students of color.

I started by recruiting students of color for a spring break trip I was leading to Washington, DC. On that trip, living and learning together, genuine relationships formed. I hired a

Latina as one of my student staff, recognizing that students of color needed to see people like themselves in leadership positions. She began to invite her friends to our Sunday evening program, especially when we focused on issues important to people of color such as the Black Lives Matter movement, understanding privilege, and Latin American liberation theology.

I worry, however, about tokenizing people of color or using them to give the appearance of racial diversity without a genuine commitment to change: the lone African American recruited for the committee, the Latinx candidate interviewed only to meet the institution's diversity requirement. I have to ask myself repeatedly if I am reaching out or seeking their friendship only because they are a person of color. Or is my motivation to build diverse relationships driven by a deeper desire to change, to embody the justice in which I say I believe?

Where I live (a small town in the rural Midwest) and where I used to work (a small liberal arts college that struggles to recruit diverse faculty and staff), there are fewer people of color with whom I can connect. So I have sought to diversify my Facebook friends and my Twitter feed. When I attend conferences where connecting and networking are encouraged, I seek out professionals of color. My world—my work life and social life—is still majority White. But as I learn, I grow more confident in intentionally seeking diverse relationships. I know that I will still make mistakes, that my privilege will always blind me and trip me up, but I am more confident in my ability to not react defensively, to apologize when I need to apologize, and to correct my behavior.

Learning is risky. When we learn, we can uncover truths that are terribly hard to swallow, truths that are more comfortable to deny or argue away. The more I learn, the more capable I become of hearing the rage and frustration simmering in the voices of people of color and seeing how my privilege has safely and comfortably guarded me against injustices committed on my behalf. The more I learn, the more I feel the suffering that inequitable systems produce and feel the shame of being a part of the problem.

But the more I learn, the more I realize I am capable of change and of creating change. It became easier for me to stop and talk to students of color in the dining hall or walking across campus. I feared their rejection, but they welcomed my attention and desire to connect. Now that I know more about White supremacy and systemic racism, conversation is easier. We have more to talk about and more points of connection. Although the changes that need to be made oftentimes feel overwhelming and ominous, I am not powerless. I can grow in learning and understanding. I can participate in the process of liberation for myself and others.

Suggested Action Steps to Risk Learning

1. Before moving on to the next chapter, choose a book by an author of color to read. Perhaps you already know of an author of color you've always meant to read but never got around to. Read that book next. (I provide a recommended resource

list at the end of this book.) While reading, record epiphanies in a journal, questions you want to explore further, and your emotional responses to what you are learning.

2. Examine your racial habits. Visit a public place where there is a diversity of people or, even better, where you are in the minority. Sit in a coffee shop or a restaurant, walk through a public park or a Black or Brown neighborhood. While you are there, pay attention to what arises within you. How does your body feel when you are around people of color? What emotions do you experience? What thoughts come to your mind? Record all these observations in a journal. Reflect on the experience later with a trusted friend who will help you be honest with yourself.

3. Expand your social circle to include people of color. Do you know a person of color at work or in your community with whom you'd authentically like to build a friendship? Invite them to go to coffee or lunch.

4. Review your social media outlets. Can you add Facebook friends of color? Follow people of color on Twitter. Here are a few suggestions:
   · Eddie Glaude Jr., @esglaude
   · Imani Perry, @imaniperry
   · Rev. Dr. William J. Barber, @RevDrBarber

- The Real bell hooks, @bellhooks
- Deray, @deray
- Mark Charles, @wirelesshogan
- Mihee Kim-Kort, @miheekimkort
- Sage Grace Dolan-Sandrino, @thhrift
- Be A King, @BerniceKing
- Ijeoma Oluo, @IjeomaOluo

5. Search the hashtag #realizediwasblack on Facebook and Twitter, watch some of the videos, and share them on your feed.

Chapter Four

Risk Teaching

We are teachers in every moment of our lives.

—bell hooks, *Teaching Community: A Pedagogy of Hope*

As I drove on Highway 34 toward Clarion and Parker Correctional, my nerves jumped and popped. Would these guys respect me? Would they listen? I was pretty sure I'd be the only woman in the room. Could I assert my authority and control the classroom? *I'll be just fine*, I told myself as I parked in a visitor's spot. *We've got it all planned*. David, my coteacher, and I had met a few days earlier to strategize and discuss how we wanted our first class on emotional intelligence and empathy to go.

David was our college's academic dean, a reassuring partner because he had decades of teaching experience. Neither of us had taught in prison, though. The thought of being in a classroom with sex offenders weirded me out the most. I imagined them with steely, bloodshot eyes undressing me in their minds. Murderers and drug dealers didn't bother me as much. There would be a guard right outside the room to go to if I ever felt unsafe. Also, I couldn't imagine the really bad guys taking our class. Hannibal Lecter doesn't do empathy.

The officer at the front gate buzzed us through while I awkwardly juggled my keys, loose driver's license, pen, notebook, and a small bottle of hand sanitizer. I chided myself for wearing dress pants without pockets while signing in on the clipboard passed through a hole in the front office's bulletproof glass. My pen kept slipping from my pile and dropping to the dirty tile floor. Only see-through bags are allowed in the prison, and I hadn't thought to grab one. Before moving through the metal detector, I dumped all my loose things in the plastic catchall bowl. When the alarm went off—red lights flashing, shrill buzzing—I jumped. David waited patiently while I tried again and again. After my third attempt, the gate officer decided it was the decorative metal tabs on my ballet flats that were setting it off. He begrudgingly let me in.

David and I paused outside the classroom door to take a few deep breaths and observe our students, who were already in the room. Through the glass window of the classroom door, I saw the men standing around, chatting and joking in their blue prison-issue shirts and pants. Some were over six feet tall, others were shorter, but all of them appeared huge to me—like giants. They were Black or Latino except for one White man. A younger African American had a large, elaborate tattoo of a woman up his neck and face. *Was this some sort of gang tattoo?* I wondered to myself. *Was that thought racist?* My eyes skipped from man to man, then to the furniture in the room—blackboard, rickety mismatched school desks, large teacher's desk. I wasn't ready. Didn't want to go in. But David opened the door of the classroom and stepped aside to let me through. *Ladies first? Really, David? Now?* I took a deep breath and walked through the door. The men all stopped talking and stared.

Whether in a prison, church class, or a book club, all teaching is risky. When a person shares information, thoughts, beliefs, and experiences with another person, this sharing naturally opens the opportunity for that person's information, beliefs, and experiences to be questioned, challenged, critiqued, and countered. The role of the teacher, then, is innately vulnerable. Although it feels risky and uncomfortable, vulnerability itself isn't bad. In fact, it's the only posture that leads to meaningful dialogue and genuine relationships. But how we respond (and how others respond to us) within that vulnerable teaching position determines the transformative power of the moment.

For four years I had struggled to teach a White male student at our college who triggered intense feelings of frustration and anger within me. He was a literal black-and-white, right-or-wrong thinker who could not (or would not) entertain a perspective different from his own. Every encounter with Brad was stressful and usually ended in me raising my voice at him in anger. I felt like I couldn't control my emotions or my reactions to him. In one memorable conversation about immigration and undocumented people in the United States, he could not understand my belief that we should support immigrants desperate for opportunities in our country. He just kept repeating, "But they come here illegally. They're breaking the law." "Yes, they are breaking the law," I responded, "but what if the law is unjust or needs reforming?"

Nothing I said, though, could open him to consider a different view. Adrenaline would rush through me during our encounters, afterward leaving me physically shaking and unable to let the conversation go. I'd rerun it in my mind, thinking of things I should have said, arguments I could have made. I also mourned how I just couldn't seem to help Brad. I felt unqualified to be his chaplain. By the end of his four-year college career, I had grown so frustrated that I gave myself permission to believe he was a lost cause, closed myself off from him emotionally, and shut down any new opportunities for dialogue.

Our dominator culture is dangerous, bell hooks writes, because there must always be a superior and an inferior party (think patriarchy, White supremacy, heterosexism, and so forth). Being socialized into such a dominator culture makes it our emotional default mode, especially when things get risky or when we are feeling vulnerable. After studying hooks, I now see that my problem with this White male student wasn't my arguments and analysis. I still believe this student's views were legalistic and dehumanizing. Instead, my problem was how, in the teaching moment, I was hard and uncompromising. The anger surging in me made me feel powerful and righteous. I sought to dominate and overpower this young man instead of teach him.

Often teachers fear losing control of the classroom (or of themselves) when emotions rise in the midst of challenge. Out of this fear, teachers seek to reduce the risk of teaching and make the classroom "safe." Typically, hooks writes, this is done by the teacher shutting down opportunities for challenge, lecturing for the entire period, and only allowing students to speak when called upon. Paulo Freire, author of *The Pedagogy of the Oppressed*, refers to this style of education as a "banking system" in which students are merely passive consumers and teachers are the depositors of information. This authoritative teaching style emerges out of our dominator culture, which, hooks writes, "encourages us to choose safety instead of risk, sameness instead of diversity."[1] In what they believe is a safe, neutral classroom, many of the White teachers with whom hooks works report concerns that their non-White students do not speak. But a classroom where the only valued perspective is the teacher's and the only culture represented is that of the dominator is far from neutral or safe for marginalized students.

Lauded as a master teacher, bell hooks encourages a different approach to teaching. She asks teachers to risk a radical openness, to engage students in dialogue and critical thinking, and to foster a democratic classroom environment where no one dominates, not even the teacher. When the teacher walks into the classroom at the beginning of the semester, it is her job to nurture a community of learners. Everyone in this community is responsible for contributing to the education of the class; every member is expected to speak, share, and be heard; every voice is valued for the perspective they can add. In a hooks-style classroom, students might keep learning journals that they periodically read out loud. Or students might be asked to contribute questions or topics of discussion to the class from assigned readings. In this class setting, the teacher focuses not on safety but on the community's shared commitment to learning and growth.

When I'd toured Parker Correctional earlier, I'd seen a teacher lecturing while sitting behind a large desk in one of the classrooms. Even before I'd read bell hooks, this posture didn't feel right to me—too authoritarian. David and I planned to sit with the students in a large circle.

When we entered the classroom, the students' desks were already arranged in a circle, so I chose the closest one. It wobbled under me as I sat. One of the inmates, a tall, lean man with a long, well-trimmed beard, stood up immediately and said, "No. Take my desk. It's better." His desk was three down in the circle, but he hoisted it easily in the air, made a quick exchange, then nodded for me to sit. Slipping into the seat, I looked up and smiled gratefully at my new friend for this kind gesture of respect. His desk was definitely sturdier and a welcome support.

After all the men had found their way to their seats and gotten situated, I compensated for my insecurity by asserting my authority (and my dominance) and introduced myself with all my credentials. "My name is Reverend Doctor Teri

Ott. I've been an ordained Presbyterian pastor for over twenty years, and now I serve as a college chaplain."

The men sat quietly listening and staring. So I continued my self-important speech.

"My job at the college is a lot like your prison chaplain's. I am there to meet the religious and spiritual needs of a very diverse community."

More silent staring. I needed to stop talking.

"David?"

David introduced himself, more humbly, then asked the men to pull out their assigned readings: two chapters from Walter Moseley's novel *Always Outnumbered, Always Outgunned* and Tony Judt's essay "Night." When we developed this curriculum, we were told some of the men would only have an eighth-grade education. So we chose readings that we didn't think would be too difficult but would help them enter and empathize with the lives of the characters. Moseley's novel features a character named Socrates, a newly released felon trying to remake his life.

I began by asking our students to summarize the plot of the two assigned chapters in their own words.

"We can do better than that," said Jarek, a dark African American whose posturing suggested he saw himself as the leader of the class. "We can summarize the whole book, if you want."

I was confused. *What did he just say?*

"We read the whole book," Jarek clarified.

David and I glanced at each other, shocked. In what classroom do you assign two chapters and the students choose instead to read the whole book? In spite of our initial fears, this classroom was quickly turning into the ideal learning community.

Animated by the energy in the room, David stood up to scratch on the blackboard about the Socrates of ancient Greece and discuss why Moseley would have chosen this name for his main character. The conversation bounced from there. The men deeply resonated with Moseley's Socrates and his desire to make something of his postrelease life. They also empathized with the dark struggles Socrates experienced, trying to control his anger when confronted unjustly by police officers. He was a large, strong African American man whose size and criminal history bred mistrust.

Two hours flew by as we talked about the novel. These men had so much to say and share that David and I just let the conversation flow. Our plan as teachers quickly transformed into a plan that included the students—their voices, their desires, their commitment to the classroom community's education. Jarek spoke about his anger as a young man and how his gang flamed his fire for violence. "I hope I get the chance to go back someday and show them the man I have become," he said.

Turell, whose voice was calm and deep, almost Zen-like, talked about how angry he was when he was first locked up: "You've got a lot of time to sit with yourself in here. And I guess I just realized that all that anger was eating me alive; it was killing me. Eventually, I made peace with myself and my past."

Quenton, whose gray hair made him appear the oldest, spoke about how violent the prison used to be. "It's better now," he said, "but it used to be predator versus prey in here. Either you were going to be the predator, or you were going to be the prey. And you didn't want to be the prey. So you manned up. You made sure you were the strong one."

With twenty minutes left before the guard would rap on our door and begin to move the men out, I shifted the discussion to the essay by Tony Judt. I had added this essay to our curriculum because Judt painfully and specifically describes what life is like for a man whose ALS has paralyzed him from the neck down: "During the day I can at least request a scratch or a re-placement of my limbs—since enforced stillness for hours on end is not only physically uncomfortable but psychologically close to intolerable. But then comes the night."[2] I thought the essay would help the men empathize with a person's struggles wholly different from their own. But one line at the beginning of the essay concerned David. As we sat in his office two days before we would teach, David pointed to the sentence on the photocopy of "Night" that lay between us on his desk. "What about this?"

I leaned over the copy to read, "In effect, ALS constitutes progressive imprisonment without parole." "Oh, I didn't even catch that," I said. "Do you think we shouldn't use the essay?" I imagined Judt's comparison to prison angering the men, and I didn't need anything more to worry about.

David thought for a minute, then said, "No. Let's use it and see what they say. We're there to learn too, and I think we'll know pretty quick if it doesn't work."

Again, the guys surprised us. Chad, the one White man, raised his hand. My chest tightened, and my heart pounded hard. Chad had not said anything yet but listened to every word of the discussion, leaning forward in his desk as if ready to pounce. His intensity creeped me out. "Yes, Chad?" I asked cautiously.

"This essay really moved me. I stayed awake all night thinking about it."

"Yeah," DeShawn jumped in. "It was written in a way that we could really feel what he went through every night."

"I can't imagine not being able to move, not even being able to scratch an itch on my own," Chad said.

All of them nodded in agreement. They'd gotten it.

The guard rapped on the door. "Time to move out."

The men stood up obediently; packed up their papers, books, and pens; and headed toward the door. But before they left, each stopped to shake David's and my hand. They purposefully looked us in the eye and said, "Thank you. Thank you for coming. Thank you for coming here to teach us."

We stood there for a moment after they had all left, paralyzed by the experience. These men were unlike anything I had imagined. Finally, I turned to David. "Wow. When do students thank their teachers like that?"

"Never. It never happens," he said, laughing.

"Was that anything like you thought it would be?" I asked.

"No," David said. "They defied all my expectations."

What I experienced in this first prison class changed me. Not only did it begin to break down many of my racist stereotypes and expectations, but I also witnessed the transformative power of a democratic teaching style where the humanity of each student is honored. In the prison environment, where dominator culture reigns supreme, where men are referred to by their number rather than their name, where they must learn to survive as predator to avoid being the prey, our students were hungry to be acknowledged as human beings. In spite of my fears and slips into dominating teacher mode, these men jumped at the chance to be heard and recognized. Ironically, it was a group of incarcerated adult males who made me feel safe to be a better, more vulnerable teacher.

The transformative power, then, of bell hooks's style of teaching is in the stance of the teacher—not as dominator or controller but as a leader of a democratic learning community based on an ethic of love. Much of hooks's work is grounded in this love ethic, which, she writes, is lived out through care, commitment, respect, and knowledge. Our culture of domination is a culture of lovelessness and dehumanization, where one always has to be superior over another deemed inferior. Living from a love ethic is a way to rebalance these relationships. "The choice to love," hooks writes, "is the choice to connect—to find ourselves in the other."[3]

As I reconsider my interactions with Brad, I wonder how our conversations would have gone had I embraced my love ethic rather than defaulting to my dominator culture. How could I have better loved this student, cared for him, and sought to understand how he had come to his views? What anxiety and fear led him to embrace a dominator culture that dehumanized desperate immigrants? Could we have connected through a more caring conversation about shared fears as White privileged people? To whom could I have introduced him so immigration would be not an abstract issue but a human one? I regret not acting from the love ethic I believe in as a Christian. But I am not alone. hooks, who describes herself as a Buddhist Christian, writes that "there is a gap between the values we hold and our willingness to do the work to create a more just society."[4] Jesus stood up to the Roman Empire with a love ethic, but we are afraid to challenge our dominator culture, afraid to face power armed only with love.

Late in her career, bell hooks accepted a job teaching at a small Methodist university in Texas that was predominantly White. The college had recruited her to help them with issues of diversity.

Before she left the university, the dean affirmed the success of her time among them, saying, "Having you come here with your unique talents for teaching, for dialogue was vital to us. Teachers here want to help students challenge their assumptions, deconstruct them, and then reconstruct them in a different way. This is what teaching is about—not just giving information but taking us inside—changing us from the inside out."[5]

This dean spoke of the transformative power of education—something David and I experienced in that first class at the prison—where boundaries of difference are crossed and assumptions challenged, deconstructed, and then reconstructed with better information. This is the ecstasy of a great education—teaching that transforms and liberates us from destructive patterns, habits, and structures. "Moving through [our] fear, finding what connects us, reveling in our differences; this is the process that brings us closer, that gives us a world of shared values, of meaningful community,"[6] says hooks. It's a process of transformation for both student and teacher alike. Never, in fact, have I learned more than when I am teaching. Teaching (also writing and preaching) forces me to articulate what I know and reflect more critically on what I have heard or read. I often ask students to lead programs or preach in worship because the pressure of leading engages them more deeply in the material and encourages them in their learning.

As you read this chapter, you might be thinking to yourself, *OK, this is all interesting, but I'm not a teacher. No one's going to show up to learn anything from me.* Even if you're not a teacher by profession, though, bell hooks says, "we are [all] teachers in every moment of our lives."[7]

Teachable moments arise constantly in life: moments when you and your friend's conversation turns to an issue about race or injustice and you discover that you each have a different take on the topic; moments when a family member says something you know or believe to be wrong and, even though you are scared to disrupt the family event, you feel the need to speak up; moments when a friend or colleague is struggling and in need of help or advice; moments in a Sunday school class or a working group when you are assigned to discuss a topic with people who hold more conservative or more liberal views than yours.

When these moments arise, we have decisions to make. First, will we risk teaching? Even though that teaching will put us in a vulnerable position? And if so, how will we teach?

Will we enter the moment with radical openness, seeking to love and connect with the other, not dominate them? Will we risk crossing boundaries, revel in differences and diversity, be willing to honestly and humbly examine our assumptions, stereotypes, and prejudice? Will we risk building connections with people who are different from us? Will we risk meaningful community?

Suggested Action Steps to Risk Teaching

1. Speak in love. When you find yourself in a conversation with someone with whom you disagree (in person, not on social media), center yourself in the love ethic and risk asking some questions like "Can you tell me more about that?" or "How did you come to this perspective?" Be genuine in your asking. Seek to understand. Then risk sharing your own perspective and how you reached it.

2. Organize a book club. Gather a group of friends to read and discuss a book together. Book club discussion guides can be found on the internet for many texts, and if you choose a literary text (such as a book by James Baldwin or Toni Morrison), curricula on how to teach them can often be found as well.

3. Volunteer to teach a class or workshop. Many faith communities encourage their members to lead and teach. Community organizations such as Rotary and Kiwanis also welcome guest speakers or teachers. Design a class or a workshop on a topic about which you've read and would like to think more deeply.

Chapter Five

Risk Following

Only the oppressed who, by freeing themselves, can free their oppressors.

—PAULO FREIRE, *Pedagogy of the Oppressed*

A group of Latina students volunteered to cook an authentic Mexican dinner for my weekly religious life program, where we typically fed about twenty-five college students. I'd designed this program to have dinner served promptly at 4:00 p.m. so students could eat and then gather for the discussion, speaker, or movie, which would begin by 4:30 p.m. We concluded by 5:30 p.m., because that's when students began leaving, slipping out to attend other meetings or programs that began at 6:00 p.m. After many years of trying to find a good time and format, the 4:00 p.m. to 5:30 p.m. time slot on Sunday nights worked, and attendance had grown.

As I contemplated the students' offer, I questioned whether they could pull it off. Cooking dinner for twenty-five isn't easy. Having the meal ready on time takes organization and planning that I doubted college students could handle. I usually paid for catering or ordered pizza. But I wanted to give them a chance.

On the day of the program, the young women were excited to share their food with our group. They were also excited to be together in the kitchen. They took their time, enjoyed one another as they prepared the food, and didn't watch the clock. Four o'clock came and went. At 4:15 p.m., I had to sit on a couch in the corner of the room full of hungry, waiting students; wrap my arms around myself; and rock back and forth, desperately seeking more patience. One thing I'd learned about building programs: consistency is key. If I didn't consistently serve dinner at 4:00 p.m., students would start showing up later. If dinner ran long, I'd have to cut a planned speaker short or reschedule our discussion on gun violence. I'd lose the educational opportunity I was using good food to lure students toward.

It took everything I had that Sunday to let go of my plan and let the Latina cooks take the lead. Dinner was finally ready by 4:30 p.m. It was delicious. We enjoyed ourselves over dinner and cut the program short. I can't even remember what our program was that Sunday. I do remember how proud these students were to share their culture's food—the smiles on their faces as we ate.

As much as it challenged my type A personality, this experience was good for me. I needed—and still need—to learn how to relax, take a step back, and embrace a different way of leading. It was also good for the students who cooked for us. They needed me to sit my butt in a corner and let them take the lead. They needed to teach me that time spent building relationships was as important as time spent building knowledge. We don't become leaders if we're never given or never take opportunities to try to lead.

In an interview for *Psychology Today*, Maya Angelou shared, "We may encounter many defeats, but we must not be defeated. It may even be necessary to encounter the defeat, so that we can know who we are. So that we can see, oh, that happened, and I rose. I did get knocked down flat in front of the whole world, and I rose. I didn't run away—I rose right where I'd been knocked down. And then that's how you get to know yourself."[1]

Anyone who knows me now as a leader and a pastor wouldn't have recognized me in 1998 when I first started in ministry. Before you can be ordained a pastor in the Presbyterian Church (USA), you have to be examined on the floor of your sponsoring church body to ensure you are theologically fit for ministry. This means getting up in front of a group of about two hundred pastors and church elders to state what you believe and respond to questions. In seminary, my friends and I referred to this process as one of the many hoops we had to jump through to become ministers that felt more like fraternal hazing than an examination of our theological fitness. It was terrifying. There were always one or two old, male ministers who liked to get up and grill the newbies, asking them really difficult theological questions, seeking more to humiliate and patronize than examine. I was twenty-five years old when I took this step toward ordination. I was also still struggling with shyness and an anxiety disorder that had yet to be diagnosed.

Before being called to the floor, I felt myself losing it emotionally. My heart pounded in my ears, my breath quickened, and tears leaked from my eyes. I crept away from the sanctuary where the meeting was being held to a small chapel off the church's narthex. Sitting in the second row, my forehead resting on the back of the wooden pew in front of me, I dissolved into what I now know was a panic attack. I heaved and sobbed as quietly as I could, afraid of being discovered in such a weak state, afraid of being humiliated in front of two hundred people, afraid of failing in front of my parents, who were there along with elders and pastors from the church in which I'd grown up.

My panic ebbed and eventually waned, leaving me emotionally and physically spent. I recovered enough to walk myself out of the chapel and back to the sanctuary, where I was soon called to come forward.

My body didn't feel like my own as I walked myself toward the pulpit. Adjusting the microphone, my hands shook. As I spoke, my voice—usually loud and overly enthusiastic—came out small and weak, so much so that I could tell people were straining to hear me. I couldn't muster any more volume, so I leaned in, my lips grazing the foam ball covering the microphone. Slowly and haltingly, I shared my carefully rehearsed statement of my beliefs. After I finished, my heart again fluttered in panic as people rose to stand in line at the microphone on the floor where they would ask me questions. I don't remember any of the questions or any of my answers, except one. A man approached the microphone and asked, hesitantly, "You seem to have trouble speaking in front of people. How do you think you'll manage preaching and teaching or other tasks of ministry that require you to speak in public?" My face flushed hot with shame. I didn't know what to say to this man's question of my obvious failure. I finally eked out, "Yeah, I'm better one-on-one with people."

Surprisingly, I passed that exam. Or they passed me in spite of my poor performance. The sanctuary must have been full of grace that day.

We tend to hang on to our failures more than our successes, and that moment of shame will always be burned in my memory. Afterward, though, I made huge strides in my growth as a pastor. Learning how to manage my anxiety was pivotal. So was being affirmed by mentors for gifts I didn't realize I had—like writing, storytelling, and most surprisingly, public speaking. These mentors gave me opportunities to try to test these gifts. I stood up in a pulpit and preached sermon after sermon. I didn't always do well. But in time and with more and more practice, I grew in ability and confidence. As a female pastor, not all doors were open to me. But I was given more opportunities in my progressive church to grow in leadership than I had ever imagined for myself.

People of color need the same opportunities to grow in leadership. In his book *Where Do We Go from Here: Chaos or*

Community?, Martin Luther King Jr. advocated for Blacks to be their own spokespersons and the leaders of their own organizations. "White liberals must understand this," King wrote. "It is a part of the search for manhood. It is the psychological need for those who have had such a crushed and bruised history to feel and know that they are men, that they have the organizational ability to map their own strategy and shape their own programs."[2]

King's words in the 1960s rose from the lack of opportunities for Black leaders in this country. We've made progress since then, but our country's leaders remain predominantly White. In 2016, US Census statistics show the eighteen-and-older population was 79 percent White.[3] Yet according to a summary of statistics gathered by Robin DiAngelo in 2016–17, the leaders and influencers of our nation were more White than the population:

US Congress: 90 percent White

US Governors: 96 percent White

Top military advisers: 100 percent White

President and Vice President: 100 percent White

People who decide which TV shows we see: 93 percent White

People who decide which books we read: 90 percent White

People who decide what news is covered: 85 percent White

Teachers: 82 percent White

Full-time college professors: 84 percent White[4]

More doors are opening for people of color to become leaders, but we privileged Whites need to ask ourselves some tough questions before our democracy can reflect and represent all its people.

In his book *Pedagogy of the Oppressed*, Paulo Freire describes the role of allies as fundamental to the struggle for liberation. People of privilege bring significant power and influence to the liberation movement. But, Freire warns, they also bring with them "the marks of their origin: their prejudices and deformations, which include a lack of confidence in the people's ability to think, to want, and to know. They talk about the people, but they do not trust them; and trusting the people is the indispensable precondition for revolutionary change."[5]

Freire's words gave me pause. Especially the part about trust. I immediately thought of the colleagues of color I worked with at the college. Although I wanted to support them and their work on behalf of marginalized students, I struggled to trust that they could do their job and lead well.

I had my reasons. Some of them—*they overtalk, aren't concise, and aren't careful to avoid mistakes*—were unique to my colleagues. Others were extrapolated to "all Black people" by my own bias. *They aren't as educated as they should be. They don't have the right experience.* When I risked following the Latina students who wanted to cook for our program, it was easier for me because they were students. Failure is an acceptable part of the learning process. But if my colleagues of color failed, I found myself thinking, our college community and our students wouldn't be served as they should or could be.

Here, I was at war with myself. The work of supporting marginalized students was so important and needed on our campus. I had seen and heard from these students about the help they needed to succeed at a predominantly White institution. When my colleagues of color failed to mobilize the community in making necessary change, I wanted to help. I saw their mistakes, and I believed I could do the work better. At times I jumped in, stepped on the toes of my colleagues, and took over.

I now recognize my behavior as paternalistic and indicative of the White savior. The term *White savior* is used to describe White do-gooders who jump in to help or "save" people of color with little regard for the work already being done, the cultural context in which the work needs to be done, and the agency of the people to know what they need and create change for themselves. This White-savior mentality has been used to describe White activists who jump in front of Black leaders at protests, White volunteers or missionaries who travel to developing nations to "civilize" or "help" the natives, and feel-good Hollywood movies like *The Help* and *The Blind Side* in which Black stories are told through White-savior protagonists.

Saul Alinsky's philosophy of community organizing has been used to create systemic social change since the 1930s. His work is based on trusting and following the oppressed members of a community. In his book *Rules for Radicals: A Pragmatic Primer for Realistic Radicals*, Alinsky writes, "It is the schizophrenia of a free society that we outwardly espouse faith in the people but inwardly have strong doubts whether the people can be trusted. These reservations can destroy the effectiveness of the most creative and talented organizer."[6] Alinsky focuses on organizing rather than on building a movement because movements come and go. Everyday people need consistent support and strategic planning to create change. Alinsky also focuses on "bottom-up demands" rather than high-profile national issues. In his model, residents are brought together through existing community institutions (such as churches, mosques, and synagogues) to discuss their needs and find common ground for action. Small victories, such as getting a stop sign placed at a dangerous intersection or forcing a landlord to make necessary building repairs, build confidence among the people in their own democratic power, leading them to seek and organize for more change. He writes, "It is when people have a genuine opportunity to act and to change conditions that they begin to think their problems through—then they show their competence, raise the right questions, seek special professional counsel and look for the answers. Believing in people is not just a romantic myth."[7]

Alinsky's rules for grassroots community organizing, which have been studied alongside the nonviolent strategies of Mahatma Gandhi and Martin Luther King Jr., helped the United Farm Workers improve living conditions for Mexican Americans in California, helped Black residents in Chicago's Woodlawn neighborhood fight exploitative landlords, and guided the early organizing work of Barack Obama.

Freire's words and Alinsky's practices call me to account. I have to risk following my colleagues of color, to trust them in knowing, better than I, the needs of marginalized students and how those needs could be met. My efforts to "save" them might make me feel good about myself (look what a good person I am!), and my work might provide a quick fix to an immediate need. (Or, it might not. White saviors tend to presume success.) But it will only breed more mistrust between my colleagues and me—relationships that could be better nurtured as collaborative partnerships instead of as a hierarchy. "Saving" my colleagues of color also perpetuates a White dominance over the ways our communities are led. If I follow their lead, they, like any other leader, might fail. But we all need sanctuaries of grace, places where we can fail up to grow and learn as leaders. These leaders might also succeed in making us White privileged people reconsider how leadership opportunities are shared. Either way, following their lead opens me (and my community) to new ways of leading and doing the work before us.

A few years ago, I learned about the national White Privilege Conference organized and led by Black leaders. In his opening welcome, founder Dr. Eddie Moore Jr. shared how as a Black man, he never imagined himself hosting a national gathering on White privilege. Yet here he was. I had brought a diverse group of students to my first White Privilege Conference. The Black and Latinx students loved it. "Eddie doesn't code-switch," they said. Code-switching is "switching" from your natural, cultural language to the language of others so you will fit in and not be ostracized as different. "It's like he's just himself," the students shared about Moore, "which makes me feel like I can be myself."

I, on the other hand, felt completely out of place. This conference was unlike any I'd attended. There were aspects I loved: the music was fun, an MC introduced every speaker with an improvised rap, and—most shocking—White men didn't dominate the question-and-answer time at the microphone. Other aspects challenged and disoriented me. Conference leaders practiced a radical inclusiveness in which everyone was expected to introduce themselves and share their pronouns. Countless times I forgot this pronoun gesture and needed to be reminded, which was embarrassing. The large multistall bathrooms were reassigned as "Gender-Neutral" with posters taped over the "Men" and "Women" signs. The first time I went, I paused, not sure which bathroom to choose. As I cautiously entered, the first thing I saw was a man at a urinal. Horrified, I dashed into a stall. *What if I had known that man? What if he had been a colleague from my group?*

All this was challenging, but the worst was the schedule. There was a schedule. But nothing ran on time. Relationships and relationship building were more of a priority than timeliness. The Black leadership laughed this off, and by the end of the conference, I laughed too. I still showed up on time for everything, but I'd stopped checking my watch every five minutes and enjoyed more conversation with others while we waited.

Freire writes, "It is only the oppressed who, by freeing themselves, can free their oppressors." When White people mistrust leaders of color because of our own prejudice, we dehumanize and devalue them. But as Freire points out, we also dehumanize and devalue ourselves. Acts of oppression make the actors inhumane: "As the oppressed, fighting to be human, take away the oppressors' power to dominate and suppress, they restore to the oppressors the humanity they had lost in the exercise of oppression."[8] The oppressors become more fully human when they follow the oppressed.

Now known as a poet of "witness" and for her work highlighting human rights abuses with groups such as Amnesty International, Carolyn Forché had no idea what was in store for her when, as a twenty-seven-year-old living in Encinitas, California, she decided to follow an El Salvadorian stranger. In January of 1979, Leonel Gómez Vides showed up at Forché's house to recruit her, as an American writer, to witness the US support for a Salvadorian government that was brutalizing its people. In spite of all the rational reasons telling her that it was a crazy and dangerous thing to do, she risked following Vides to El Salvador. There, she was immersed in a country and a people seeking liberation from corrupt dictators, horrific violence, human rights abuses, and misguided US intervention. Forché listened to Vides when he told her "the power of the poor to change the course of history is the world's one hope" and followed him to meet peasant farmers, the country's dictators, US ambassadors, and even Archbishop Oscar Romero. The young poet who went to El Salvador did not return, Forché later wrote. The woman who *did* return was wholly new and more fully human. In her memoir, *What You Have Heard Is True: A Memoir of Witness and Resistance*, she concludes that it was as if Vides "had stood me squarely before the world, removed the blindfold, and ordered me to open my eyes."[9]

Newly dedicated to documenting human rights abuses, Carolyn Forché began her work of "witness," a woman testifying to what she had seen and been shown, injustices that would go overlooked if not brought to the world's attention.

In creating the proposal for this book, I recognized my need to risk following people of color. I needed to be liberated from a lifetime of being influenced by predominantly White people, White communities, and White leadership. I also confronted my biases that keep me from trusting valuable colleagues and leaders who can oftentimes teach me new and better ways. The key to my liberation, I recognized after reading Freire, is trusting and following the oppressed. Following can help me become more fully human.

As I wrote, I thought about all the White male theologians I read in seminary—John Calvin, Karl Barth, Reinhold Niebuhr, Paul Tillich—and wondered why I hadn't dug more into James Cone, Ada María Isasi-Díaz, Cornel West, or Delores Williams. When I recognized my habit of reading and listening to predominantly White scholars and writers, I realized I was simply consuming the resources and the thinking most readily presented to me through the media and my own circles of influence. Once I became conscious of who I was following (and not following), I intentionally sought to change.

My commitment to risk following is why each chapter of this book is centered on the work and writing of a thought leader of color. These leaders were not hard to find once I committed to decentering White voices. At first, I thought this commitment would feel limiting. Instead, it has introduced me to books and people I would never have discovered otherwise, broadening my interests and my understanding.

To risk following people of color is more than expanding a reading list though. I feel different having lived into this commitment. The world feels more open to me, the ways of learning, of seeking and creating change, more numerous. I am less rigid, more flexible and open. I see the gifts of people of color more readily. I see my own gifts more clearly as ways to contribute through collaborative partnerships and mutuality.

Freire would say I am being freed to become more fully human.

Suggested Action Steps to Risk Following

1. Consider the organizations in your community that are led by people of color and what they are working on. How can you plug into their work and offer your help as a follower?

2. Create a book club with a group of friends dedicated to reading authors of color. Use my recommended resource list to choose your books.

3. Research the candidates up for election in your state, county, or community. Are there any people of color running? Reach out to them. Get to know their views and their story. Find ways to support their candidacy.

4. Visit a religious community led by people of color. Before you visit, do your research to make sure you know how to follow cultural and religious rules of etiquette. Use Stuart Matlins and Arthur Magida's book, *How to Be a Perfect Stranger: The Essential Religious Etiquette Handbook*, as a guide.

Chapter Six

Risk Leading

Society needs nonviolent gadflies to bring its tensions into the open and force its citizens to confront the ugliness of their prejudices and the tragedy of their racism.

—MARTIN LUTHER KING JR., *Where Do We Go from Here: Chaos or Community?*

The Black, Latinx, and LGBTQ+ students at my college were finding ways to tell their faculty and staff that our institution's systems and structures were not serving them. When they graduated, they were glad to be rid of us, of the microaggressions and racism, of being "spotlighted" in class whenever issues of race were discussed, of the constant pressure to code-switch and shape-shift to fit in at a PWI (predominantly White institution). A group calling themselves the "Unseen" surfaced the racial tension present on campus by slipping letters of protest under office doors of select faculty, staff, and administrators. I received one myself. This unnerved and upset White faculty and staff. What these marginalized students shared contradicted what we heard from our White students and assumed was true for all—that our college felt like home and our students' years with us were the best of their lives.

In their letters, the Unseen outlined their concerns about unaddressed racism and the changes they demanded. If the demands were not met, the group said, they would share their stories and complaints with the local and national news media. The group was anonymous because as marginalized students, they didn't feel safe revealing their identities. They even set up a separate Unseen email account where they could be contacted. This anonymity gave them a measure of control in a situation and a system where they had little.

"Society needs nonviolent gadflies to bring its tensions into the open," Martin Luther King Jr. wrote, "and force its citizens to confront the ugliness of their prejudices and the tragedy of their racism."[1] King's strategies of nonviolent "agitation" and protest brought to consciousness underlying racial tension—a tension that was uncomfortable for White people to face. Our communities aren't ready for this, King heard from White allies. You'll just create a White backlash, he heard. King was "gravely disappointed" with these responses, writing, "I have almost reached the regrettable conclusion that the Negro's great stumbling block in the stride toward freedom is not the White Citizens Councillor or the Ku Klux Klanner but the white moderate who is more devoted to order than to justice; who prefers a negative peace which is the absence of tension to a positive peace which is the presence of justice."[2] King wasn't afraid of tension. In his "Letter from Birmingham Jail," he referenced Socrates's method of creating tension in the mind so individuals could grow in critical thinking and analysis.[3] The tension and discomfort King surfaced were necessary for our society's transformation and growth. Serving as the president of the Southern Christian Leadership Conference (SCLC), King "gadflied" our nation's leaders.

On June 23, 1960, King met Massachusetts senator John F. Kennedy for breakfast in New York. Kennedy was running for president and wanted King's support. King decided not to endorse Kennedy—or Nixon, for that matter—saying he didn't see much difference between the two. But King was impressed with Kennedy's manner, referring to him as "honest" and "forthright."[4]

During their breakfast meeting, King pressed Kennedy on civil rights, emphasizing the movement's need for strong presidential leadership, and asked for immediate federal action to protect voting rights and eliminate racial discrimination in federally assisted housing. Kennedy promised to follow through.

King felt good after this meeting and hopeful after Kennedy was elected. But Kennedy did not seem to comprehend the nation's urgent need for racial justice. It took multiple attempts and nine months for a frustrated King to get an appointment with the newly elected president. When, on October 16, 1961, they finally met at the White House, King asked the president why he had yet to move forward with his promise. Kennedy demurred, explaining that his administration was working on it but that the political climate in Congress was not supportive of civil rights legislation. Also, Kennedy asserted, pushing for change would arouse backlash that would be counterproductive. In other words, *Not now, Not this way, Hold on, Wait.*

King was not appeased.

Knowing federal legislation was key to their success, the Southern Christian Leadership Conference set out to turn the tide of public opinion to their favor and increase the pressure on their political leaders. King wrote, "We will be greatly misled if we feel that the problem will work itself out. Structures of evil do not crumble by passive waiting. Evil must be attacked by a counteractive persistence, by the day-to-day assault of the battering ram of justice."[5]

King believed the protests the SCLC had planned for Birmingham, Alabama, would show the American public how Black people were treated in the South. Bull Connor, the infamous commissioner of public safety for Birmingham, could be counted on for vicious and disturbing violence.

As the Birmingham protests grew and images of police dogs attacking protestors and fire hoses stripping the clothes off Black bodies—including those of women and children—were shared on national television screens, public opinion on segregation began to shift. This national media attention paved the way for King to apply even more pressure for federal action and legislation.

In an interview with the *New York Times*, King declared Kennedy's record on civil rights "inadequate" and revealed plans for sit-ins on Capitol Hill and a mass march on Washington. Not long afterward, President Kennedy gave a pivotal speech on national television calling on the American people to banish segregation and racism from our land. Kennedy also said that he would be proposing a civil rights bill to Congress. With this extraordinary progress and the promise of federal legislation on the horizon, Kennedy's assassination on November 22, 1963, was devastating. Our nation was sick with violence.

But enough momentum had been built for federal civil rights legislation that all was not lost with Kennedy's death. President Lyndon B. Johnson worked with King on the legislative initiatives Kennedy started. This work culminated in the Civil Rights Act of 1964, which ended legal segregation in public spaces and banned employment discrimination.

One summer, when I was working as a counselor at a wilderness camp for girls, the gadflies (in this case, horseflies) were so bad around the outhouse that we'd sprint to the smelly pit to avoid getting bit. Horseflies are attracted to your head. They'll actually burrow into your hair to bite your scalp. To protect ourselves, we'd wear hats or wrap our hair in handkerchiefs. This helped some, but there was no escaping. The gadflies never let us relax, upsetting every chance to get comfortable. They motivated us to reach our goal, the outhouse, as quickly as humanly possible.

Leaders of good will often need to be reminded of the power they hold to create systemic change and encouraged toward this uncomfortable and risky work. I can empathize with the temptation to maintain the comfortable status quo, to avoid taking risks and rocking the boat. Leadership is lonely, and the work is hard. Difficult decisions must constantly be made, and leaders are criticized for both what they do and what they don't do. Leaders need gadflies who will consistently encourage them to do what is difficult but right. The best gadflies, like King, will bite and motivate but also foster respectful relationships with those in power—relationships where critiques can be heard as constructive calls for systemic change and not as a denigration of the leaders themselves.

In sharing their list of demands with faculty and staff who were not part of our college's senior administration, the Unseen wisely enlisted allies who could act as intermediary gadflies—people willing to use their power and privilege to ensure the students' concerns would not be dismissed.

At first our administrators were opposed to working with the Unseen because of their anonymity. *How do we know who they are? They might not even be our students. They should have the courage of their convictions and reveal themselves. This is not the right way to protest.* I and other faculty and staff considered our administrators' response—which sounded to us like *Not now, Not this way, Hold on, Wait*—and risked siding with the Unseen. We encouraged our senior leaders to listen and work with the group, reminding them that in our college's hierarchical structure, they were the ones with the most power to create transformative change.

A White male faculty member wrote a letter for our school newspaper acknowledging and validating the Unseen's charges, which led to more letters being written and brought even more tension to the surface. In response, our administrators called a town hall for faculty, staff, and students to discuss our campus climate. This discussion, where our predominantly White community openly heard the critiques and concerns of our Black, Latinx, and LGBTQ+ students, convinced our senior leaders to act. The president and his cabinet formed a Diversity, Equity, and Inclusion (DEI) team, on which I served.

I've always seen my leadership role as a minister to be both pastor and prophet. I am to comfort and care for people—but also to speak truth to power, encouraging, prodding, and challenging toward transformative change. The Bible is full of people God has called to serve as prophets. Nathan prophetically confronts King David over sleeping with another man's wife, then having the husband killed to cover up the rape. Elijah is sent by God to confront and condemn King Ahab and his wife, Jezebel, who killed their neighbor Naboth in order to take possession of his vineyard.

Playing the prophet takes a kind of courage that I do not always have. But as the feminist theologian Mary Daly said, "You learn courage by couraging." Daly's quote is taped to my desktop computer screen so I can always see it, as God consistently calls me to act in ways that require more courage than I believe I have, calling me to risk leading—even when I feel like I am the wrong person for the job.

Excuses can always be found to avoid this risky, uncomfortable work. The Bible is full of people seeking to excuse themselves from God's call to prophetic leadership. When God asks Moses to lead the Israelites out of slavery in Egypt, Moses questions God for a whole chapter and a half. *Why me? How will they know you sent me? What if they don't believe me? I'm not very eloquent. Don't you want a better public speaker?* And finally, *Please, God, can't you just find someone else?* The prophet Jeremiah also tried to get away with the "bad public speaker" excuse as well as the "I'm too young" excuse.

A colleague in ministry once told me she wasn't called to be prophetic—she was called only to provide comforting pastoral care. I was tempted to ask for her God's phone number, because my God constantly cajoles me into uncomfortable leadership positions I'd much rather avoid.

Before the Unseen activists emerged on our campus, I had organized a small group of faculty, staff, and alumni, four White and two Latinx, to attend the national White Privilege Conference, that year held near us in Cedar Rapids, Iowa. I'd heard lots of my Presbyterian colleagues lauding the conference as a challenging yet transformative experience. We attended workshops on developing skills to interrupt and challenge racism and White supremacy with love and compassion. We heard speakers on topics such as "Creating Belonging in a World of Power, Privilege, and Separation" and how racial violence, such as lynching, inflicts psychological trauma on both the victim and the victimizer in a workshop called "Exploring Post-traumatic Master's Syndrome and Embodied Racial Justice."

When our group gathered for breaks and meals, we discussed what we were learning in light of our campus context.

Each of us felt inspired to share. On our van drive home, we decided to lead a postconference seminar for faculty and staff and excitedly hatched our plan.

I advertised the event, coordinated our A/V support, and ordered food and drinks to entice people to come. Each of us agreed to take a different part of the presentation. We also agreed to break attendees into small groups to discuss a handout I had brought home from a workshop with racial justice educator Debby Irving. The handout listed and compared dominant cultural values such as self-sufficiency, either/or thinking, and the glorification of "busy" to transformational values such as interdependence, both/and thinking, and the prioritization of being present with others.

As the date of our seminar approached, some members of our group raised questions. One White colleague suggested we soften our approach, saying things like, "Our community isn't ready for this yet. We shouldn't break them up into small groups and make them discuss issues of race. We shouldn't make them uncomfortable."

Hearing this hesitancy, I recalled another dominant value on Irving's list—the belief that comfort is a right, a feeling to which we are entitled. No one has the right to make you uncomfortable, we are taught to believe, even though, as Irving also named, discomfort leads to growth. With this in mind, I responded to my colleague, naming the fear we were all feeling that comes when you're trying to disrupt the status quo. I encouraged them to lean into the discomfort of leadership. "I know this feels risky," I said. "But I believe our colleagues can handle this, and nothing will change if we don't try."

The room where our event would be held was on the top floor of what used to be our old Carnegie Library. It was a popular meeting room, with plush carpet, large windows, and the portraits of our college's past presidents (thirteen White men, one White woman) gazing down on us. When I pictured leading this room full of PhDs in a conversation about White privilege, my heart bucked like a panicked horse. At that time, I'd only read a few antiracism books and attended one conference. I rechecked our PowerPoint slides and rehearsed my part of the presentation, all while asking myself, "Why am I leading this?" I felt completely unqualified to be leading anyone in any sort of discussion about race. I imagined saying something stupid—or worse, racist—in front of all those smart people. I imagined being asked questions I couldn't answer. I imagined my colleagues leaving the seminar thinking it was a waste of time—or worse, that *I* was a waste of time.

But I also asked myself, "If not me, then who?" Our college has only a few faculty and staff of color. Our Office of Intercultural Life is tasked with meeting the needs of all our students from marginalized populations. My one Black colleague who staffs this office can't and shouldn't bear the full burden of educating us all. She, as a person of color, also shouldn't have to educate White people on what it means to be White. I had recognized my community's need for leadership, particularly the need for a White person to guide her predominantly White community in conversations about race. In spite of my fear, I was feeling called to step up and do more.

"Thank you all for coming. Please feel free to stick around, enjoy some food, and talk some more." I closed our presentation with relief. The small group discussions had been productive, and now I was gratified to see people clustering afterward to keep talking. There were aspects of the event we could have improved. My fear of being asked questions in front of the whole group or of looking and sounding stupid led me to avoid discussion as a whole. This opportunity would have been valuable, and I knew I was avoiding it, but I'd allowed myself this one safe "out" to keep myself up front in leadership. Perhaps our dominant culture's habit of either/or thinking also leads us to assume an all-or-nothing approach to action. But small steps forward are OK. If you want to try bungee jumping, you don't have to start by leaping into the Grand Canyon.

After this experience, I risked leading more, but never alone. I partnered with other faculty and staff, convincing them that their leadership on these campus issues mattered, that caring about an issue is not always enough, that we have to step up front when others don't or can't.

After two years, our DEI team worked to revamp our curriculum to include more diversity education, examined our process of responding to incidents of bias and discrimination, and developed trainings to increase our community's cultural competency. Our work was not perfect and far from complete. But we saw a growing awareness of the need for change and a new willingness to dedicate energy and resources to the work.

When we ponder the risk of leadership, we likely imagine ourselves in front of a crowd with no one else to rely on for support or strength. But the most effective leaders—such as Martin Luther King Jr.—understand the power of shared leadership and coalition building. Leading does not mean going it alone.

Taking after King, the Reverend Dr. William Barber's work in North Carolina reveals the change that can be created through powerful partnerships and coalitions. Inspired by North Carolina's history of "fusion politics," a national phenomenon of the 1890s where different political parties cooperated and coordinated their efforts to address issues of common concern, Barber gathers and inspires people from all sides of the political spectrum and with various agendas to work together.

In his book *The Third Reconstruction: How a Moral Movement Is Overcoming the Politics of Division and Fear*, Barber describes how he mapped out all the different "justice tribes" in North Carolina that had organized around particular issues, including access to health care, voter suppression, criminal justice reform, or environmental abuse. Talking to each of these "tribes," he convinced representatives to attend a "People's Assembly," where they formed a massive statewide coalition.

"We learned something important," Barber writes about the gathering. "Though our issues varied, we all recognized the same forces opposing us. What's more, we saw something that we hadn't had a space to talk about before: There were more of us than there were of them."[6] In 2006, the People's Assembly coalesced around a moral agenda and created a fourteen-point list of issues they wanted their state leaders to address. Then they organized a series of marches, where thousands gathered on the steps of the state capitol in Raleigh to present their agenda. These "Moral Monday" protests became so large that they garnered the attention of the national media. Barber's coalition of "justice tribes" was committed to gadflying their political leaders until the People's Agenda became the agenda of North Carolina's government. Their first crucial win expanded early voting and made same-day registration possible, key legislation enabling people who didn't have a day off on Election Day to participate in the political process.

We don't know how many people are on our side until we risk standing up. We don't know how many people will partner and work with us until we risk leading.

In 1968, King wrote, "The white liberal must escalate his support for the struggle for racial justice rather than de-escalate it. The need for commitment is greater today than ever."[7] If King were still alive, he would continue to emphasize the need for White liberals to risk leadership. The risk, the vulnerability, the stakes of leadership frequently led White moderates to tell King *Not now, Not this way, Hold on, Wait.* King always responded to these suggestions by prophetically pushing back, saying, "If not now, then when?"

To those of us who see the cycle of indifference, the avoidance of risk and discomfort, the measures used to maintain the unjust status quo, I can also hear King ask, "If not you, then who?"

Suggested Action Steps to Risk Leading

1. Identify the communities to which you belong. What needs within these communities call to you? Gather a group of community stakeholders to discuss the issue and brainstorm solutions. Leave the meeting with an action plan of concrete next steps.

2. Examine the power structures you participate in—your local government, your workplace, your church or faith community, your school system. Who has the least power in these structures? What can you do to amplify those voices?

3. Examine the leadership in your community. Who are your leaders? What gender are they? What race? What religion? What political affiliation? Compare the demographics of your community to the leadership demographics. Who is represented by your leaders? Who is not? Who needs to be encouraged to take on a leadership role? You? Others?

4. Who is being told *Not now*, *Not this way*, *Hold on*, *Wait* in your community? How can you serve as a gadfly to motivate leaders to act? How can you support the gadflies already advocating for change?

Chapter Seven

Risk Listening

White man, hear me!

—JAMES BALDWIN, "The White Man's Guilt"

What can a Black person say that would help a White person hear and understand systemic racial oppression? "It is difficult," writes W. E. B. Du Bois. He shares the following parable, which I have adapted:

> Imprisoned in a dark mountainside cave, a person peers out to see people walking by. The prisoner calls to the passers-by, speaking courteously and persuasively, telling them about all the souls who are imprisoned with him; people hindered in their natural movement, expression, and development;

and how setting them free would not only be sympathetic and helpful but liberating for all.

The people passing by don't hear the prisoner, though, or feign as if they don't hear. Sometimes they cast a curious glance but never pause long enough to consider the prisoner's plea.

This frustrates the prisoners, and more begin to speak up. They raise their voices. They gesture wildly. They cry out to be noticed but begin to feel as if there is some sort of invisible plate glass between them and the world. Why can't the free people hear them?

More people notice the prisoners now. But they don't understand what the prisoners are saying, and the wild gesturing seems a bit silly. Funny even. They chuckle to themselves and walk on.

This makes the prisoners hysterical. "They're laughing at us!" they begin to scream and hurl themselves at the invisible plate glass. Realizing they will not be set free, they are determined to break free. A few raging souls successfully shatter the glass, crashing through bloodied and disfigured, only to find themselves at the feet of a horrified mob, threatened and afraid for their very existence.[1]

As I contemplated what to include in this chapter, I asked myself, *Who can I talk to about their Black experience? Whose story can I share in this chapter on listening?* I remembered a student who attended my Sunday evening religious life program. Dontae captivated me with her strength and beauty, a self-described "Black warrioress" on social media. I could count on her to never keep quiet. We often discussed issues of social and racial justice on Sunday evenings, conversations where Dontae would hold forth, her leadership evident among her peers. I remember one tense moment when the group was discussing the All Lives Matter response to the Black Lives Matter movement. Dontae called out the White students in the room who weren't contributing to the conversation: "Why aren't you saying anything? Why are you just sitting there expecting us [the Black students] to do all the talking?" Dontae's question hung in the air until one White student finally mustered the courage to respond.

As I do with many of my students, I followed Dontae's life after college on social media. *I could reach out to her,* I thought to myself. *I could see if she'd allow me to interview her for my book.*

Then I caught myself. This didn't feel right. What was I missing? Where was I going wrong?

Du Bois's cave parable serves as a reminder that marginalized people have been speaking to us for centuries. They have been trying, in every possible way, to get the attention of the privileged who walk by. But we have not listened. The parable also powerfully reveals the psychological, spiritual, and physical cost marginalized people pay as they speak, protest, and finally rage to get our attention. It wasn't right for me to interview Dontae if asking her to share her Black experience meant ignoring those who were already speaking.

117

I didn't need to talk to Dontae. I didn't need to ask her to extend her precious limited energy on me. There were plenty of people, plenty of resources, to listen and learn from.

No matter what question a White person has about the Black experience, some marginalized person has already put energy into answering it. As one of my queer students likes to say, "Jesus is your friend, and so is Google."

Ijeoma Oluo started blogging about the Black experience after Trayvon Martin, who was the same age as Oluo's son, was killed. Her blog turned into the best-selling book *So You Want to Talk about Race*, where she answers questions such as Why am I always being told to "check my privilege"? What is cultural appropriation? Why can't I touch your hair? Why can't I say the N-word?

Instead of calling Dontae, I revisited a collection of essays by James Baldwin.

"White man, hear me!" Baldwin wrote in August of 1965, an explosive time in America. In February, Malcolm X was assassinated. In March, John Lewis led six hundred peaceful protestors over the Edmund Pettus Bridge in Selma, Alabama, where, to the nation's horror, they were brutally attacked and beaten by state troopers. On August 11, the Los Angeles Watts neighborhood exploded in response to police abuse.

Baldwin's essay "The White Man's Guilt" calls on White people to be honest with ourselves—to stop claiming we do not see what we see or hear what we hear and to stop whitewashing history as a way to reassure ourselves that we are good, moral, and innocent.

For much of my life, growing up in predominantly White surroundings, I wasn't listening to Black Americans because I didn't know any personally. I was forty-one years old when the Black Lives Matter movement emerged, revealing how a young Black boy (Trayvon Martin) carrying a bag of Skittles was seen as a threat. The man who shot him (George Zimmerman) was acquitted on grounds of self-defense. I was forty-three years old when I finally prioritized reading books by thought leaders like James Baldwin. Half a lifetime passed before I heard and recognized myself in the White waitress who refused to serve Baldwin at the diner.

Before I was even born, Baldwin was speaking against racial injustice, gesturing wildly like Du Bois's prisoners to catch the "White man's" ear. His prose resurfaces every time our nation's brutal history manifests itself in the daily news.

In February of 2020, Ahmaud Arbery was shot and killed while jogging through a White neighborhood. Baldwin is quoted by the *Atlantic*: "Not everything that is faced can be changed, but nothing can be changed until it is faced."[2]

In May of 2020, George Floyd suffocated under the knee of a Minneapolis police officer. Baldwin is quoted by *Berkeley News*: "When you try to slaughter a people and leave them with nothing to lose, you create somebody with nothing to lose. If I ain't got nothing to lose, what you gonna do to me?"[3]

In January of 2021, White nationalists were empowered to violently and successfully storm the US Capitol. Baldwin is quoted by Facing History and Ourselves: "American history is longer, larger, more various, more beautiful, and more terrible than anything anyone has ever said about it."[4]

The continued relevancy of Baldwin's words reveals a nation stuck in a cycle of systemic abuse—a nation full of powerful, privileged people who expect to be heard when we speak but fail to listen when confronted with truths that require us to change.

"Embedded in our white identity is a sense of entitlement," writes professor of Christian and social ethics Anna Marie Vigen. "White folk tend to assume we are knowledgeable, rational, skilled individuals." We expect to be heard and quickly become indignant if we are not. Those of us who are highly educated and/or from upper-middle and upper socio-economic classes are also "used to a certain 'authority' and agency,"[5] Vigen adds, leading us to approach conversations as if we were experts rather than as ready listeners without expectations or preconceived ideas. This White enculturation, or White entitlement, must be unlearned in order to learn. We need to recognize and acknowledge our numerous, reflexive habits of not-listening. Here are a few I am seeking to unlearn.

Listening with an Agenda

"I hear what you're saying, and I'm going to apply the parts of it I understand to my goals, my plans, my idea of what is right. I will shape your narrative to fit my own."

I had a reason, a goal for a possible interview with Dontae—material for my book. If our conversation veered away from my agenda, I would have been tempted to steer her back to my purpose. If her words didn't quite fit what I needed, I would have been tempted to make it fit. I know I'm guilty of this form of not-listening, which is painful but necessary to acknowledge. Listening without an agenda means letting go of control over the conversation. This, I confess, is a real struggle for me. Within the conversation, I have to constantly stop myself—sometimes even physically shaking my head free of my agenda—in order to open myself to where the other person wants to go. I have to be willing to follow another's lead in a conversation to risk listening.

Listening to Co-opt or Translate Another's Story into Your Own

"I hear what you are saying, and I understand because I've experienced something similar. Listen to my story."

In the moment, it might feel compassionate to respond with examples of what we believe are shared feelings and experiences. Such commiseration might be valuable if the conversation centers on shared experiences of racial, gender, class, or sexual identities—two Black women seeking support from each other, two trans men, two middle-class White males. But if a White woman of privilege tries to compare a Latina woman's story of struggle to her own, this "similarizing" of stories diminishes or neutralizes the differences between the two—differences that the White woman of privilege can and should acknowledge. Focusing on shared feelings also projects accountability elsewhere. The implied message being, "We're the same. The world is the same for both of us. Therefore, I don't need to change. Someone else does."

Listening to Dismiss or Gain Ammunition for a Counterattack

"I heard what you were saying. Now listen to me tell you why you are wrong."

There's a difference between a reasonable exchange of ideas, where people of goodwill discuss complex problems in order to come to the best solution, and a conversation where a person's only intention is to dismiss or argue away the other's point. As I explain in chapter 4, "Risk Teaching," bell hooks describes this as a danger of our dominator culture, where there must always be a superior and an inferior party. The goal in these conversations is to win the argument, not find the best solution or a peaceful path forward.

As the DEI team on our college campus got into the thick of our work, amplifying the voices and concerns of our marginalized students, we met resistance from a few White male faculty. They listened to all the reasons diversity and inclusion initiatives were good for our community, then counterattacked, saying that by prioritizing the voices of the marginalized, we silenced the voices of others. If diversity is such a benefit to our community, they argued, shouldn't all voices and all views be heard equally? Their critique felt like a trap because it was—a trap meant to get us second-guessing our important work, stall our progress, and dismiss our efforts to listen to those who have not traditionally dominated and controlled our campus conversations.

Listening to the Tone of What Is Said Instead of the Content

"I heard what she was saying, but she shouldn't have said it the way she did. She should have used a more respectful tone."

The increasing frustration of Du Bois's prisoners is apparent. As the people pass by, ignore, and fail to hear, the imprisoned people's emotions rise. They cry out, they rage, they beat against the glass wall. Imagine being in that emotional moment of built-up frustration and hearing the response, "I'm not going to listen to what you have to say right now because you're not being polite."

A meme went viral on social media revealing how White supremacist society dismisses Black voices no matter how they are expressed. Centering on a photo of a mob gathered around a burning car, the photo's caption read, "Why can't you protest peacefully?" Then it showed a photo of a peaceful Black Lives Matter march with the caption "No, not like that"; a picture of NFL players taking a knee with "No, not like that"; and a picture of NBA players wearing black T-shirts with "I Can't Breathe" across their chests and the caption "No, not like that."

"Tone policing" is dismissing a person's argument or words because, to the listener, the tone used was inappropriate or impolite. Tone policing is frequently used against Black women, accusing them of being inappropriately loud and angry.

Audre Lorde's response to racism is anger. In her essay "The Uses of Anger: Women Responding to Racism," she writes,

"I have lived with that anger, ignoring it, feeding upon it, learning to use it before it laid my visions to waste, for most of my life. Once I did it in silence, afraid of the weight. My fear of anger taught me nothing. Your fear of that anger will teach you nothing, also." Lorde goes on to share an experience at an academic conference where she was speaking out in anger. A White woman responded, saying, "Tell me how you feel but don't say it too harshly or I cannot hear you." Lorde questioned this response: "Is it my manner that keeps her from hearing, or the threat of a message that her life may change?"[6]

I'm learning to unlearn my habits of not listening—habits that have protected me from painful truths but have also inhibited change that would have fueled my growth. The counseling classes I have taken and the therapy sessions from which I've benefited have taught me that painful truths cannot be ignored if we ever hope to find our way to health, healing, and wholeness. This applies to our social lives as well. We cannot ignore other people's experiences of us, their words of protest, or their truth telling if we want to live in a healthy society. Knowing this has led me to learn new and valuable ways to risk listening.

Be Present

One of my favorite group activities focuses on active listening. I split the group into pairs and give one individual in the pair a prompt to respond to, such as "Talk about a time in your life when you felt proud of yourself" or "Talk about a time when you felt vulnerable." While one talks, the other is instructed to listen carefully, without interrupting, without making any kind of noise, until the person has finished sharing. Then the person who listened is to report what they heard the other say. I prompt them to focus on not only the words their partner used but also their body language and tone of voice. What did your partner communicate? What did you hear them say with their words, their posture, their eyes, their tone? When we finish, someone usually confesses, "Wow. That was hard!" The exercise leads us to discuss how difficult it is to listen and be truly present with another person yet also how valuable it is. In just a few minutes of focused, active listening, we learn a lot about each other.

Develop a Double Consciousness

In her essay "To Hear and Be Accountable: An Ethic of White Listening," Vigen describes the "double consciousness" that people of color develop in order to survive in a White supremacist society. People of color need to understand and be conscious of the White way of living and behaving in order to navigate, survive, and succeed in the dominant culture. But they also need to cultivate an understanding of themselves that is not dependent on, or "infected by," a White society that disparages color.

Before taking a group of students to a conference, I was asked by a Latina what kind of clothes she should pack to wear. I wasn't exactly sure, I told her, but I assumed the dress would be casual. She pressed me to get more information.

She needed to know specifics: "What does 'casual' mean at this conference? Can I wear blue jeans, or would black pants be better?" At the time, I didn't understand why she was so focused on the conference's dress code. But the trip prompted good conversations about race, which led the Latina student to share more. She explained that it was important for her to know the expectations so she could fit in, so she could dress in a way that was culturally appropriate. As a Latina, this meant dressing appropriately White so she could successfully navigate the White conference space.

Listening to this Latina student, I learned about her unique struggle. My experience of White college students is that they couldn't care less about what they wear. They will show up in sweatpants and a hoodie unless I specifically tell them to dress otherwise. The need to navigate between two cultures—to be doubly conscious of both Latinx and White ways of interacting—is foreign to White people who live, work, and study in White spaces.

According to Vigen, White individuals need to develop a double consciousness in order to better listen across boundaries of race: "White people need to cultivate the skill to be fully present in interactions with people of color, while also being able to step back from the immediate dialogue in order to be cognizant of the larger picture and to check one's self."[7] This requires a mindfulness, an attentiveness to what is happening within you and without. If you are paying attention to a Black woman who is speaking and you notice feelings of anger or guilt arise within you or you feel the need to "check out," go silent, or react defensively, attend to those internal responses. *Why am I feeling this way? What is triggering these feelings in me? What White narrative or White habit is keeping me from hearing what this woman has to say to me?* Clearly, this is a lot to be conscious of in a single moment. Resmaa Menakem, a psychotherapist who specializes in racialized trauma, suggests excusing yourself from the conversation, if needed. Pretend like you have to use the restroom or get an eyelash out of your contact. Just find some reason to take a break, breathe, and check in with yourself before reengaging. People of color are more skilled in the use of their double consciousness than White people because they need it to survive and thrive in a White-dominant culture. White people can develop this skill as well. But it requires commitment.

During the 2021 Super Bowl, an ad, sponsored by Jeep, featured Bruce Springsteen in the "middle" of America talking about our nation's need to heal from deep political divisions and polarization. Springsteen preached his message of reconciliation in front of a small chapel in rural Kansas, the Christian cross overset with an American flag, before climbing in his Jeep to drive away.

I mostly tune in to the Super Bowl to watch the commercials. When Springsteen came on, I paid attention—I've listened to his songs on repeat, screamed my lungs out at his concerts. Seeing Springsteen, an American icon, tramping around the snow of rural America felt good to me; it felt right. I didn't give it any more thought.

Afterward, I caught a discussion about the ad on social media. Friends were criticizing the commercial for centering Whiteness—or more specifically a White Christian male—as the American norm, the "middle" where all Americans should meet. The commercial's scenes of a White male in rural Kansas in front of a white chapel evoked nostalgic feelings of "Americana"—rugged, pioneering, faithful. I, as a White middle-upper-class woman from the Midwest, felt comfortable with this commercial. As I develop my double consciousness, I grow more uncomfortable with my unquestioned feelings of comfort triggered by White supremacy.

Decenter Yourself; Center the Marginalized and Their Human Experience

In chapter 5, "Risk Following," I describe how my life centered Whiteness. I studied White theologians in seminary, read books by White authors, surrounded myself with White friends, lived in White neighborhoods, attended White churches, worked with and hired White employees. In order to risk listening to marginalized voices, I needed to redirect my perspective of Whiteness as the metaphorical "middle" or the center by which all others are defined. White supremacy, or White "centered" ways of being and living, are so embedded in my life and American culture, it feels as if an exorcism is needed to extract its power over us. Once we recognize the hold White supremacy has, though, small steps can be taken to break it down and replace it with new knowledge, new ways of living and being in the world.

Jocelyn and I wanted to celebrate the success of her mujerista theology study group. We went shopping together for food that Jocelyn's Latina group members would enjoy.

There are three grocery stores in our town. I shop at the two that carry more high-end items and organic produce. But Jocelyn directed me to the Save-a-Lot, where people who needed to be more price conscious shopped. I was paying for the food out of my budget, and I wanted to celebrate. I was so excited about the success of Jocelyn's group, about the theology they had studied, the way they had grown together and supported each other. "Let's celebrate big!" I said. But as we wandered through the aisles of the Save-a-Lot and I kept wanting to throw more and more in our grocery cart, Jocelyn just shooed my choices aside with a flick of her hand, saying, "No, Teri. Not that. It needs to be simpler." "Simple living," she kept repeating to me as she selected one package of Abuelita chocolate, a gallon of milk, some *galletas*. She did let me drive her to the Mexican bakery in town, though, where she chatted for a few minutes in Spanish with the owner before selecting a few pastries. I kept wanting to buy more, but Jocelyn insisted we had enough. "We don't want to waste," she asserted. "We can always get more if we need it."

From Jocelyn I learned about the hospitality of her Mexican culture. Everyone, the whole community, is invited to your birthday party. If you run out of food, you go get more. If you have food leftover, you invite people over the next day to finish it up.

Following Jocelyn around that grocery store, centering her culture's hospitality, the prioritizing of relationships and community, made me reflect on my White cultural practices, seeing them in a new light. In my midwestern White culture, I'd try to carefully plan the right amount of food for the right number of guests. Leftovers would get packed up for my family to enjoy later or sent home with guests. There is more than one way to host a great party. No race or culture should be upheld as the one "supreme" standard. To recognize and embrace this multicultural view breaks down "supremacist" thinking, or the assumption that the familiar practice of hospitality is the right practice. Decentering Whiteness opens us to a whole new world of possibilities.

James Baldwin writes on behalf of not just Black Americans but Whites as well. White Americans have "impaled" themselves "on their history like a butterfly on a pin," suffering and struggling against their "personal incoherence." "They are dimly, or vividly, aware that the history they have fed themselves is mainly a lie, but they do not know how to release themselves from it." They "become incapable of seeing or changing themselves, or the world."[8]

We cannot continue to walk by Du Bois's prisoners, assuaging our guilt with false theories of White racial supremacy; false theology that White people were created more pure, more in the image of God; myths of White fragility, of White women needing to be protected from the dangerous Black man. We cannot continue in our ways of not-listening for the sake of *our* liberation as well as those who are marginalized. Listening to diverse voices, entertaining multicultural perspectives, is the key to broader possibilities and complex problem-solving.

If we White privileged people can risk listening, a new story can be written by us all, one where every human is valued, every culture respected, and every voice heard. A story that doesn't end like Du Bois's parable, with bloodied and disfigured prisoners breaking through to our horrified feet. But a story of the violence, and the rage, and the pent-up frustration of the imprisoned cave dwellers never escalating because those who dare to hear risk listening.

Suggested Action Steps to Risk Listening

1. Create a list of questions you have about the Black experience or a culture different from your own. Research those questions on the internet. Partner with a friend to share what you learn.

2. Dedicate an evening or two to watch movies or a series about the Black experience, such as *I Am Not Your Negro*, *The Black Church* on PBS, or *Black Is, Black Ain't*.

3. Read op-eds or other articles of cultural criticism by writers of color, such as Roxane Gay, Ijeoma Oluo, Austin Channing Brown, Charles Blow, and Eddie Glaude Jr.

4. Read Eddie Glaude Jr.'s 2020 bestseller, *Begin Again: James Baldwin's America and Its Urgent Lessons for Our Own*, to understand the relevancy Baldwin's words still hold as well as how we have yet to hear him.

Chapter Eight

Risk Speaking

A time comes when silence is betrayal.

—MARTIN LUTHER KING JR., *A Testament of Hope: The*
Essential Writings and Speeches of Martin Luther King, Jr.

I didn't know any out gay people until I went to seminary.
There was a student at my college who might have
been gay, or not. It wasn't OK then to be out. But when I
arrived at my Presbyterian seminary in 1994, fresh out of
college, everyone was debating whether or not a "practicing
homosexual"[1] could be ordained as clergy. Our community of
pastors-to-be was divided on the issue. The debates I observed
were hot and righteous. I didn't have an opinion at the time;
I'd never even thought about gay rights before. So I just listened to the debates, not knowing enough to participate. But
the controversy led me to study the seven Bible passages used

to condemn gay sex and eventually conclude for myself that there wasn't sufficient support for such judgment. This was a safe position to take at the time—my seminary leaned liberal.

After I graduated from seminary and my "liberal bubble," I recognized that the larger church debate leaned more conservative and antigay. My position wasn't comfortable or accepted anymore. For the next ten years, as the debate over LGBTQ+ inclusion raged in my Presbyterian denomination, I remained silent. I preached regularly, but fear kept me from taking any sort of stand or declaring myself on anyone's side. When church leaders gathered for quarterly regional assemblies to hash out the politics and polity of our denomination, my fear of looking and sounding stupid kept me from speaking up. The larger the crowd, the less likely I was to say anything at all.

I beat myself up for my silence. I knew awareness wasn't enough. I wanted wisdom and eloquence to come from my mouth, moving myself and others toward change and inclusion. Wise, eloquent words would have been great, but even a stumbling I-don't-know-what-to-say-yet-but-I-am-listening-and-I-will-try-to-figure-out-what-I-need-to-do-or-how-I-need-to-change would have been better than silence. Because my silence, I have come to learn, not only burdens those left to interpret it but also makes me complicit in systemic oppression.

Elie Wiesel's acceptance speech for the Nobel Peace Prize both haunts and inspires me. In the speech, Wiesel remembers a young Jewish boy from his time in Auschwitz. "Can this be true?" the bewildered boy asked his father. "This is the twentieth century, not the Middle Ages. Who would allow such crimes to be committed? How could the world remain silent?" Wiesel responds to this boy's question in his speech, swearing never to be silent when and wherever human beings endure suffering and humiliation. "We must always take sides," Wiesel said. "Neutrality helps the oppressor, never the victim. Silence encourages the tormentor, never the tormented."[2]

It's important to understand that silence in the face of oppression of any kind is not empty, it is not neutral. It is not nonaction. Saying nothing in the face of systemic oppression supports that oppression.

"A time comes when silence is betrayal."[3] On April 4, 1967, in New York City, Martin Luther King Jr. broke his silence on the Vietnam War at an assembly of three thousand hosted by Clergy and Laymen Concerned about Vietnam (CALCAV). Before this moment, King had struggled with the decision of whether to speak publicly against the war. He had been sharply criticized for passing comments he'd made that were picked up by the news media, and his own advisors were divided on whether King's antiwar stance was wise. Some encouraged him to speak. Others told him it would weaken the civil rights movement and distract him from his main work on behalf of Black Americans.

King made up his mind on a January flight to Jamaica, where the civil rights leader intended to get some rest. The January 1967 issue of *Ramparts* magazine caught his attention. As he got settled for the flight, King picked up the magazine and flipped through its pages until he reached the story "Children of Vietnam." One photo showed Vietnamese children who had been horrifically burned by American napalm. Another showed a Vietnamese mother holding her dead baby. King was sick.[4] His silence on the war betrayed all he held sacred: his stance on nonviolence, his activism against injustice, his call as a preacher of Jesus's gospel, his commitment to the dignity and worth of every person.

He decided to do everything he could to end this war.

I decided to begin speaking about LGBTQ+ inclusion after my husband challenged me to break through my fear. It was the summer of 2008, and I was serving as the pastor of a small church in North Carolina. My church's pews were filled with people in favor of LGBTQ+ inclusion, a few against, and plenty who'd rather not discuss it. The influences of the Bible Belt were also all around us. I was considering doing some sort of sermon series, but I couldn't come up with a topic interesting enough to carry through four or five weeks of summer. I was discussing some of my bad (and safe) ideas with my husband when a wry smile slowly stretched across his face.

"You know what you should do?" He was animated and excited.

"No, what?" I replied dryly, knowing his grin meant trouble for me.

"You should do a series on difficult texts and topics. Pick the Scripture texts and the topics pastors typically avoid, and preach on those. You could do Abraham sacrificing his son

Isaac. Cain and Abel. That horrible passage in Psalms where they pray for their enemies' babies to be dashed against the rock. Revelation. And you should definitely talk about gay sex and sexual orientation."

"What? You're crazy." I was already hyperventilating. But my husband's challenge lay there like an invitation to an ex-boyfriend's wedding. Something I knew I didn't want to participate in but probably should.

I took on Dan's challenge, preaching on Cain and Abel, which turned into a sermon about capital punishment. I preached on the story of Abraham sacrificing Isaac, a story I have never been able to justify—and I decided not to justify it in my sermon, only point out its problems. I preached on the end times and Revelation. (I skipped the baby bashing. Feel free to read it for yourself—Psalm 137. It's awful.)

Finally, I took on what the Scriptures say about gay sex. Ensuring I couldn't back out of the challenge, I advertised the texts and topics on which I was planning to preach in the church's newsletter and weekly bulletin. My congregation of one hundred came alive with energy and attentiveness. Our discussions about the topics lasted long after Sunday morning worship. But my church members were most abuzz when their pastor talked about gay sex, a topic many told me they'd never heard addressed from the pulpit. Friends were invited to come specifically for my sermon that Sunday, and every pew was packed full. Apparently, lots of people wanted to hear what I had never publicly said before.

Each sermon in this series was an extraordinary challenge. My fear and anxiety motivated me to work harder than I ever had. My goal was to preach in a way that could be heard by all, even if they disagreed. But I was also determined to be clear about where I stood on these issues. It's easy for a pastor to justify not taking a stand by saying that he or she has to preach to "both sides of the aisle" or to be everyone's pastor. But as Wiesel warns, such neutrality only serves the status quo. Staying safely in the middle, neither for nor against, doesn't challenge the speaker or the listeners to grow toward just living and faithful thinking.

When the Sunday arrived for my much-anticipated final sermon, I locked myself in my church office minutes before worship and began to collect myself. My windows overlooked the parking lot, and as I paced back and forth in my black preaching robe, I watched the people arrive. It felt like everyone in town, not just the regulars, was streaming into my church that day. My heart thudded in my ears. I put my earbuds in and played a song I'd been listening to on repeat from the *Power of One* movie soundtrack, dancing around to the music like a boxer preparing for a fight. I had no idea how the people who filled the pews would receive my words. I prayed for God to use me for good and to get me through this.

I felt like throwing up.

Once in the pulpit, it took a few minutes of preaching to shake my nerves off and find my groove. But the church was more attentive, quieter, and more focused than I'd ever experienced before. This fueled me, and my passion built as I moved through my message. As I walked them through the seven Scripture passages that refer to gay sex, I heard them flipping the pages in their Bibles to read and follow along.

Many Christians simply assume that the Bible is clear on the issue of gay and lesbian sex. That's what they've heard or been taught, but rarely have they studied the Scriptures for themselves. In 1993, after years of deadlocked debate, our Presbyterian denomination approved and encouraged a three-year period of study of sexual orientation in our congregations. But when the three years were up, less than 3 percent of Presbyterian churches reported having engaged in any kind of study. In fact, one highly placed Presbyterian official was even quoted as saying, "My grandma told me it was wrong, and that's good enough for me."[5]

My goal was to encourage people to dig deeper, to examine the texts for themselves, to make it clear that the Bible is *not* clear about the lives and relationships of LGBTQ+ today. I thoroughly complicated the seven texts, explaining their historical and cultural context. When read carefully, the sin of Sodom in Genesis 19 was a severe violation of the sacred and cultural obligation to offer hospitality to strangers and travelers. The overly quoted text from Leviticus 18:22, "You shall not lie with a male as with a woman; it is an abomination," is part of the Holiness Code of Israel, a set of regulations meant to distinguish the Israelites from their foreign neighbors.[6] This Holiness Code also includes putting children to death for being disrespectful to their parents, putting adulterers to death, and more menial prohibitions against wearing clothes of two different materials, against tattoos, against shaving and trimming your forelocks (what we refer to as "bangs"). It's pretty ridiculous to argue for one of these culturally bound regulations to be upheld while ignoring all the rest.

In the New Testament, sexual orientation or gay sex is never mentioned in any of the four Gospels. But Paul, writing from a Greek culture where it was common for men to have sex with adolescent boys and for men to prostitute themselves to other men, condemns such behavior. In Romans 1, Paul specifically addresses the sins and sinners of the Greeks: envy, strife, deceit; gossips; those who were boastful; those who rebelled toward their parents; those who were foolish, faithless, heartless, ruthless; women who "exchanged natural intercourse for unnatural" and men who, "giving up natural intercourse with women, were consumed with passion for one another" (Rom 1:26–27). In other letters from Paul, specifically 1 Corinthians and 1 Timothy, where his words have also been used to condemn gays, the original Greek is unclear and highly debated, with no consensus among scholars on Paul's actual meaning.

For Christians who hold to the authority of Scripture, Paul's words are challenging. But all words, even those inspired by God, must be read in context. What Paul did not know in his day was two adults of the same sex living together in a monogamous and consensual relationship. Paul also had no concept of sexual orientation. While we can discern Paul's view about Greco-Roman gay sex from his words in Romans, we cannot determine all things. The Bible does not clearly speak to what we know about sexual orientation and same-sex relationships today.

Knowing that there were people in the pews and a large portion of my denomination who would disagree with me, I concluded my sermon by making it clear on whose side I stood. I encouraged my parishioners to focus on the broad biblical themes of love, justice, forgiveness, and grace rather than on specific passages. And I turned them to the life and ministry of Jesus, whom we Christians are called to emulate.

I concluded my sermon with these words:

> In discerning how I should behave toward gay or lesbian people in today's world, I remember Jesus. I remember Jesus reaching out in love and grace to the foreign Samaritan, Jesus reaching out in love and grace to the diseased leper, Jesus reaching out in love and grace to the paralytic, Jesus reaching out in love and grace to the blind man, Jesus reaching out in love and grace to the shunned woman with many husbands, Jesus reaching out in love and grace to the oppressed, and the persecuted, and the marginalized. I remember Jesus reaching out to all those who were considered by his culture to be "sinful" or "different" or "unclean."
>
> I remember Jesus when I hear stories like Matthew Shepherd's, who was brutally beaten and left for dead in Colorado because he was gay.
>
> I remember Jesus when I think about the young gay teenager who hears the whispers behind his back at school, who puts up with all the condescending jokes about gays during the day but who cries himself to sleep at night, afraid to tell anyone how he really feels, afraid to tell anyone who he really is.
>
> I remember Jesus when I hear on the news that Bishop Gene Robinson, the first openly gay bishop in

the Episcopal Church, had to wear a bulletproof vest to his consecration because he had received so many death threats from his fellow Christians.

I remember Jesus when I hear that my gay friend has been chased down and tormented by a homophobic gang of boys looking for a little "fun."

I remember Jesus when I consider the millions of gay and lesbian people who are hungry to live and serve in Christian community but who do not feel welcome in the church because we have sent them the message that the Bible clearly says no to them.

To my surprise, this sermon series was one of my finest experiences of the church. Afterward, no one told me I shouldn't have done it. Everyone agreed that the church should be speaking out about issues that matter—even if doing so was controversial and disruptive to the comfortable status quo.

A few people asked for copies of my sermon on welcoming gays and lesbians. For the first time in my life, I had written something that was shared so widely that I started getting emails and messages from people I had never met. Most of the messages were positive. People thanking me for speaking up. People sharing that they had a son or a daughter who was gay who'd never heard a word of welcome from the pulpit. Other messages were from people who disagreed with my interpretation of Scripture. And a few people left the church. They just slipped quietly away, which made me sad. I would have appreciated the chance to talk before they made their decision to leave.

I learned a lot from this experience. When you risk speaking, the consequences can be painful. But I'd come to a point where staying silent in the face of known oppression is the more difficult burden to bear.

The risk King faced in speaking against the Vietnam War cannot be underestimated. King knew the FBI had been tracking his personal life and worried they might incriminate him if he criticized the government. Advisors also warned him that a public antiwar stance would jeopardize his relationship with President Lyndon Johnson and the civil rights work they had already accomplished. But King was undeterred. He made his speech, calling on the Johnson administration to halt all bombing in Vietnam and to work toward peace negotiations.

The backlash was quick and condemnatory. Only a few newspapers and magazines supported King. The *Christian Century* boldly declared his speech "a magnificent blend of . . . political sagacity and Christian insight, of tough realism and infinite compassion."[7] But most media portrayed King as irresponsible and irrational, as a leader who had injured his influence and that of the civil rights movement. The NAACP announced that King's merging of the civil rights movement with the peace movement was a tactical mistake. King's call for peace negotiations to be conducted with the Viet Cong, North and South Korea, the USSR, and China also led to intensified FBI interest in his "communist" sympathies.

On a more personal level, old friends refused to comment on his speech. Others dissociated from King. He was tired, living out of a suitcase, getting four hours of sleep a night. The pressure was intense. "I saw your picture in the paper, Martin,"[8] one NAACP leader needled, insinuating King's antiwar efforts were to meet his ego's need.

In response to these consequences, King said, "I was politically unwise but morally wise. I think I have a role to play which may be unpopular. I really felt that someone of influence has to say that the United States is wrong, and everybody is afraid to say it."[9]

Once you start speaking, it's difficult to slink back into silence. A few months after I finished my sermon series on difficult topics and texts, I was contacted by a group of pastors who were trying to get our church's polity amended to welcome gays and lesbians into the leadership roles of officers and pastors. They'd read my sermon and invited me to speak at our next large assembly, when the new polity would be voted on. Just like when my husband suggested the sermon series on difficult texts and topics, I panicked.

I had a legitimate excuse not to speak. Pregnant with our first child, my due date fell within weeks of the assembly meeting. Leaving early in the morning to drive my overstuffed, uncomfortable, and uncaffeinated body two and half hours to the meeting, sitting in an unforgiving wooden pew to listen to long debates, and then participating in that debate with my normal anxiety heightened by hormones was the best description of hell I could imagine. But now that I had broken my silence on LGBTQ+ inclusion in the church, I felt obligated to keep speaking. Even though it took every bit of courage I had to preach once on this issue, it wasn't enough, and it wasn't about me. I could pat myself on the back for that one sermon, feeling all brave and proud of myself. But unless I lived into that courage and kept speaking when opportunities arose, my one moment of courage wouldn't amount to much. Thirty-eight weeks pregnant, I drove to the assembly meeting.

It was a warm early fall day in North Carolina, and the air conditioning in the church sanctuary was broken. Everyone fanned themselves with their meeting papers and dockets as we lined up at two microphones set up facing the chancel. One side in favor of changing our church's polity to be more inclusive of gay and lesbian leaders. The other side against. With hundreds of people at this meeting, the line at each microphone stretched to the back of the large sanctuary and snaked along the back wall. It was going to be a long, hot, uncomfortable day whether you were pregnant or not.

It felt like I waited in that line to speak for hours. As I slowly inched forward, I couldn't focus on anything anyone else was saying at the mic because I was rehearsing my speech in my head. I robotically stepped forward as a speaker from the "for change" side, then from the "against change" side finished—the black bulb of the microphone's head looming before me. Sweat streamed down the inside of my clothes. My skin broke out in hives as I imagined my voice amplified throughout that sanctuary full of hot and increasingly cranky people. But I'd done this before, I told myself. I could do it again. *Breathe, Teri.*

My turn at the mic finally arrived. "I'm thirty-eight weeks pregnant, and it is blazing hot in here." People laughed with me, and I took a breath.

> But I had to be here. I had to come and speak because I want to be a part of a church that is bold and brave in standing up for those who are oppressed and persecuted by our world. I want to be a part of a church that stands up for justice for all of God's children. I want to be a part of a church that cries out, "Different is not deficient." I want to be a part of a church that is in the world but not of the world by being a safe place for our gay and lesbian brothers and sisters to live and to serve.

I went on to share stories of gay people who I knew who were suffering and for whom the church had been of no help.

"And so, I want our polity to change," I concluded, feeling everyone's eyes on me. "I want this amendment to pass. Because I believe it will send a clear message to the world that we in the church are guided by a higher moral standard, that we are guided by the gospel of Jesus Christ, by the One who risked everything for those who are persecuted and oppressed."

As I stepped away from the microphone, I felt like I had run a marathon. My body went limp with relief and exhaustion as I practically crawled back to my pew.

After everyone lined up at the microphones had their chance to speak, we voted. My side lost that day, which wasn't unexpected. It would take two more years of speaking up and challenging the status quo before our church's polity would be changed to welcome gay and lesbian leadership.

King's speech on April 4, 1967, did not bring the Vietnam War to an end. But he kept speaking, determined not to betray his God, his call, or himself again.

King wrote, "God's unbroken hold on us is something that will never permit us to feel right when we do wrong. God has planted within us certain eternal principles, and the more we try to get away from them the more frustrated we will be."[10]

Fortunately, he had a place to go where he was understood. After his April 4 antiwar speech, King returned to preach at his home church, Ebenezer Baptist in Atlanta. He reiterated many of the points he had made against the war. Then more vulnerably, he shared, "The calling to speak is a vocation of agony."[11] Yet King vowed never to be silent on the issue again.

The church gave him a standing ovation.

No matter our role or our circumstance, our silence in the face of oppression betrays our best selves. The consequences of speaking are real. But so are the consequences of staying silent. King was eventually killed for the risks he took. But what I have read of his "buoyant" mood after that April 4 speech and the way he felt unburdened leads me to believe the risk, for King, was worth it. King's soul was free, unlike those who murdered him.

I, too, have felt liberated after taking the risk to speak in the face of oppression. We can make so many excuses for ourselves:

I'm not the right person to speak.

I don't know enough.

I should let others have the floor and the opportunity.

I'm too afraid. Too inexperienced. Too pregnant.

Even if our excuses are valid, our silence weighs on us, because we know we should risk speaking when we can. Opportunities to risk speaking open spontaneously and unexpectedly in the classroom or the book club, in parking lot conversations after church, on phone calls with family and friends, and in PTA, school board, or Rotary meetings. These moments give us pause, our conscience pricked by something someone has said that feels wrong or that we know is wrong. And yet we so quickly close our mouths and carry on, letting the moment pass. Beating ourselves up afterward. Exercising mental and moral calisthenics to justify our silence and alleviate our shame.

You don't have to be a preacher, a public leader of a movement, or a famous person with a huge platform to risk speaking. You can start today, practicing with your best friend, partner, or spouse. Speak about issues you see arising from the daily news. Work your opinions out. Read to get better informed. Write an op-ed for your local paper. Ground yourself in these practices so you can speak up when the opportunity opens, when you become aware that something is wrong or unjust.

Coax yourself out of silence, even if your voice shakes.

Suggested Action Steps to Risk Speaking

1. Practice speaking with a friend group, partner, or spouse. Listen to what your voice sounds like out loud. Raise social issues in your conversations so you can move the thoughts in your head to the words you speak. Work out your opinions in these conversations. Read to get better informed.

2. Look into bystander intervention programs and trainings. The Step Up! Program offers free resources and paid facilitated trainings where groups of people can practice speaking in a safe setting. Organize a group of friends or your faith community to work through these trainings (https://stepupprogram.org).

3. Look into nonviolent resistance training for yourself or for a community group. Check out "What Kind of Nonviolence Training Do You Need?" from the Pace e Bene Nonviolence Service for a list of great options and resources (https://paceebene.org/blog/2019/11/22/what-kind-of-nonviolence-training-do-you-need).

4. Read the resources available on the OpEd Project's website, and consider taking one of their workshops. Write an op-ed for your local paper (https://www.theopedproject.org).

Chapter Nine

Risk Failing

Our greatest disappointments and painful experiences—
if we can make meaning out of them—can lead us toward
becoming more of who we are.

—GLORIA ANZALDÚA, *Borderlands /*
La Frontera: The New Mestiza

DeShawn's boyish grin is both shy and inviting. Over six feet tall, lean, and lighter skinned than the other Black men, he is always the first to arrive at the classroom. DeShawn greets me with a handshake, his shaved head shining in the fluorescent lights, then folds his long body into one of the school desks that my coteacher and I have arranged in a large circle. I stay standing, fidgeting with the pens and papers on my desk, wishing I could check my email or look busy on my cell phone.

Small talk isn't easy in prison. Volunteers are not supposed to share personal information with the prisoners. Yet asking them what they did that day or how their cellie is treating them in the six-by-eight cement box they share feels inappropriate.

I was teaching another prison class with David, our academic dean. I can't remember the class's content or what we were discussing, but I do remember my anxiety—which is always present. I wanted to be a good teacher. I wanted to do well in the classroom and hold my own with David, who has a ton more teaching experience than I. My nerves settled some after all the men arrived and awkward small talk could be set aside, but I still sat poised on the edge of my chair, ready to prove myself as a teacher.

At one point during the class discussion, DeShawn responded to a question I'd raised in a way that was unexpected and didn't fit what I was hoping to get across. Following DeShawn's response would have taken the discussion in a different direction, a direction I was unprepared to go. So I asserted myself, interrupting him before he could finish. "No, DeShawn," I remember saying. Maybe I even put my hand up to stop him from going further. Then I redirected the conversation back to the topic I'd wanted us to pursue.

DeShawn, who had been leaning forward in his seat, fully engaged in the conversation, settled back after I cut him off. I don't remember him speaking again. He didn't disengage entirely. His face, eager to please, followed the discussion as it flowed from student to teacher to student around the cold, vast classroom that doubled as the prison's greenhouse. We strained to hear each other as our voices bounced off the cement floors and walls and vaporized over the tiny seedlings struggling to live long enough to be planted in the spring garden.

After class, DeShawn respectfully shook my hand, thanked me for coming, and wished me a safe drive home. All the men do this, eager to dispel the image outsiders have of them. DeShawn was no different. But as I left class that night, I couldn't stop thinking about him. I had no idea why DeShawn was in prison, no idea of his crime. As the gate of the prison unlocked to set me loose into the wind of the Illinois prairie, I imagined I wasn't the first in DeShawn's life to tell him he was wrong. Incarceration itself sends the message that you have failed, that you are a failure. I told myself to let it go, got in my car, and turned on some music to distract myself from the guilt that was rising like water in a bathtub I'd forgotten was running.

Privilege protects us from failure. It gives us options. We don't have to risk going to a prison or risk speaking up in the face of injustice. We don't have to risk listening to those who aren't as privileged or risk staying in uncomfortable conversations. We don't have to risk being wrong or risk having our minds changed or risk learning how we have benefited from the dehumanization and oppression of others. We make mistakes, but we don't have to risk facing them or risk making more by pushing ourselves beyond the safety and security our privilege provides.

I could face the mistake I made with DeShawn, or I could ignore it. As a volunteer, I was free to walk away from the prison, free to leave behind my teaching and the incarcerated men I've met there. Driving away from the prison the night after I'd cut DeShawn off, the discomfort of facing my inadequacies as a teacher, as a person who seeks to do good and perform well, was a feeling I wanted to flee, not face.

Gloria Anzaldúa advises otherwise. Avoiding or distracting ourselves from our inadequacies, our mistakes, our failures traps us in ignorance, Anzaldúa writes, keeping us from seeing ourselves clearly. We've got lots of defensive strategies to escape the agony of our inadequacies and mistakes. "I have used all of them," Anzaldúa shares. "I have split from and disowned parts of myself that others rejected. I have used rage to drive others away and to insulate myself against exposure."[1] She also describes how we busy ourselves in order to keep awareness at bay. We fixate on drinking, smoking, popping pills, chasing the latest self-help fad, repeating, repeating, to numb ourselves or distance ourselves or distract ourselves from the truth of who we are and what we have done.

In this state of avoidance, we need to be "arrested" or stopped in order to assess ourselves and process our experiences. Anzaldúa relies on Coatlicue, the Earth Mother goddess from the Aztecs, to slow her up so her psyche can assimilate her failures, her inadequacies. If she doesn't take the time, Coatlicue will lay her low with illness, forcing her to stop. This "Coatlicue state," as Anzaldúa calls it, this disruption of carrying on in spite of our pain and failure, is what propels the soul to do its work. "Our greatest disappointments and painful experiences can lead us toward becoming more of who we are. Or they can remain meaningless. The Coatlicue state can be a way station or it can be a way of life."[2]

Manifesting as a paralysis or depression, the Coatlicue state exposes Anzaldúa to the depth of her dissatisfaction with herself. She resists, trying to hold herself together rather than allowing herself to fall apart. She sweats, her head pounds, she's unwilling to talk to anyone, she descends into an underworld, a place of death, where she wallows, sinking deeper and deeper until, after reaching bottom, something forces her to push up, walk toward the mirror, and face what she sees. Anzaldúa describes this painful journey as a "crossing," where she is led again and again into new territory, new knowledge, new awareness. On the other side, Anzaldúa is a new person.[3]

At its best, incarceration could be viewed as a state of Coatlicue, an arrest, an opportunity to review the past, look in the mirror, and grow in soul. The first class I taught at the prison was on empathy and emotional intelligence, part of a curriculum my faculty friends and I had developed. On my first day, I began with the traditional opening invitation: "Tell me why you are taking this class."

College students respond to this invitation quickly, as if passing a hot potato around the room. For some, they are interested in the class's content; for others, the class is required for their major. There are always a few the teacher wishes weren't so honest: "This was the only class that fit my schedule."

But the class of incarcerated men, some with gray-speckled hair, answered slowly and thoughtfully, listening as each shared.

"I'm taking this class so I can learn and make a difference here with the newer guys."

"I want to make a difference too, so I want to learn and develop new skills."

"I want to contribute to my community."

"I want to be a good father to my children."

Later, our conversation turned to past regrets. Jarek spoke about his anger as a young man and how his gang flamed his fire for violence: "I hope I get the chance to go back someday and show them the man I have become."

Turell, whose voice was calm and deep, talked about his anger when he was first locked up: "You've got a lot of time to sit with yourself in here. And I guess I just realized that all that anger was eating me alive; it was killing me. Eventually, I made peace with myself and my past."

Not everyone I've met at the prison—whether part of the incarcerated population or corrections staff—has such a willing spirit. Not everyone I've met outside of prison, including myself, is willing to risk and face failure. Putting ourselves in positions where we might make mistakes, admitting the mistakes we do make rather than "saving face," can feel uncomfortably weak and vulnerable—feelings to be avoided rather than embraced as an opportunity for soul growth and consciousness raising.

At its worst, incarceration controls through frustration and failure. Once inside, volunteers quickly learn there is no way to avoid breaking rules or making mistakes.

More than two million people are incarcerated in the United States, five times more than in any other country. Our prisons are overcrowded, understaffed, and underresourced. They rely on volunteers to provide positive rehabilitative programs for offenders, who would otherwise go without. By essentially serving as unpaid staff, volunteers save the Department of Corrections hundreds of thousand dollars annually.

Despite the need for volunteers, though, the correctional system makes giving your time and talent as difficult as possible. Mistakes are a given. You will fail in this system. The policies and procedures could easily be a sketch for *Saturday Night Live*. Let's review the rules, shall we?

Background Check

1. Volunteers must provide complete job history, addresses of residences (dating back to birth), Social Security number, emergency contacts . . . in case volunteer is caught in a lockdown or taken hostage. (You don't want your husband to find out on the evening news.)

2. Describe any and all tattoos. You will be asked for photos. Yes, even the regrettable mermaid you got with friends on spring break. Submit photos

on time. Delays could result in an application being denied. Denied volunteers may not reapply. Ever.

3. Make copies of all paperwork. When the forms are lost or misfiled, they will be easier to resubmit.

4. Background checks will be processed in three weeks. Except when they take three months or a year.

Drug Test

1. Yes, you have to take one.

2. Yes, you have to urinate in a cup under the observation of an officer of the same gender.

TB Test

1. The volunteer must visit the facility's health clinic to be tested for tuberculosis—a highly contagious bacterial infection typically spread in lower socioeconomic classes due to our nation's lack of affordable health care.

2. The infectious control nurse will needle a bubble under the pale skin of the volunteer's inner forearm.

3. The volunteer's attention will be sought by the incarcerated men waiting for their appointments on wooden benches in the hallway outside. A tall, leering male will introduce himself with "Hey, baby. Whatcha' doin' here? I'm Cocaine Kitty. You remember my name."

4. The volunteer must return in two days for the bubble to be checked for inflammation, irritation, or any other infectious disease she may have caught in the facility's clinic.

Photo ID

1. The volunteer's photo must be taken for her ID badge. Put your toes on the line, turn to the right, turn to the left.

2. Please enjoy our bulletin board of celebrity mugshots while you wait: O. J. Simpson, Robert Downey Jr., Vanilla Ice.

3. The volunteer's fingerprints will be taken. All five fingers. Both hands. For cleanup, use the dirty rag hanging off a nail on the bulletin board.

Orientation

The volunteer will spend two to three hours listening to the chaplain drone through the required information. Because the chaplain is weary of this job, the volunteer must ask the most pertinent questions, such as the following:

1. What happens in a lockdown?

2. What do I do in a hostage situation?

3. Who do I go to if an incarcerated man pressures me for favors after class?

4. Which bathroom is the cleanest?

5. How do I respond when catcalled by Cocaine Kitty?

Dress Code

1. *Men* must wear long trousers and a shirt with sleeves.

2. *Women* must wear a dress, skirt, or slacks with an appropriate top. No see-through apparel (lace, netting, holes), halter tops, spaghetti straps, or tank tops (anything where bra straps can be seen). Extremely short skirts or shorts are prohibited (must be below the knee). No tear-away pants. No extremely suggestive, short, or tight-fitting clothing. No spandex, leggings, or bodysuits. No swim tops or suits.

3. Underpants are required.

Risk Failing

As I recruited and coordinated a group of faculty from our college to volunteer at the prison, time and time again, our efforts were frustrated by failure.

My busy-working-mom volunteer rushed from the gym to the prison to get her TB test in the clinic. The officer at the gate took one look at her, announced that the strap of her sports bra was showing, and sent her back to her car. *Fail.*

Late for my class, I ran to the prison gate in the pouring rain, grabbing my husband's black-and-gold Steelers umbrella from the car. Those aren't just Steelers colors, I was informed. Those are also gang colors. *Fail.* Back to the car you go.

After multiple emails and follow-up phone calls to the warden, I finally get permission for us to bring in a DVD of a movie to show as part of our class. But when it comes time for the class, the DVD player can't be found. When it is found, it's broken. *Fail.*

During this process of getting our faculty approved as volunteers, I learned that another local college had also tried to get some classes started at the prison. They eventually gave up, though, unable to jump through all the correctional hoops. I learned how disappointed the incarcerated men had been when these college classes didn't happen. Failure felt inevitable in this system. But if I didn't risk failure, I'd disappoint the men too—men whose lives were already so full of disappointment. If I didn't risk failure in this system, I'd also never grow in awareness and understanding of all that my privilege protects me from. The closer I got to those who were incarcerated (closer in both physical proximity and relationship), the more

I understood how most of them had come from social systems that were also designed for them to fail.

In 1965, Martin Luther King Jr. moved his family from Atlanta to a small West Side apartment in Chicago. King moved there to support the Chicago Freedom Movement and address racial discrimination entrenched in urban cities that kept Black people locked in ghettos, overcrowded schools, and low-paying jobs.

Only a few days after their move, Martin and Coretta noticed a change in their children's behavior. Tempers flared, and the children regressed emotionally. Their apartment was hot and crowded. Their neighborhood lacked safe, green space for play. King recognized how being poor and living in the city became an emotional pressure cooker for families, who were set up to fail in marriage, parenting, healthy child development, and more.[4]

As a professor in the African American Studies Department at Princeton University, Eddie Glaude Jr. lives in a suburban community. In his book *Democracy in Black*, he writes about calling his son out of the comfort of his bedroom to see something happening outside their home. The police were down the road at a White family's house. One of their boys had gotten into trouble, and the police were bringing him home to talk to his parents. Glaude pointed to the scene down the street, then turned to his son and, without blinking, said, "They would not have brought you home to me. They would've taken you to jail."[5] Glaude may not have wanted to go there in this moment with his son, but it's also possible that a Black boy would not even make it to jail. Black parents fear for their children's lives every time they leave the relative safety of their homes, Glaude writes, because Black people are seen first as criminals, set up to fail in a policing system not designed to protect them.

In his work and writing, Glaude calls us to a revolution of values. When people profit from the incarceration of millions, corporations make money off the sick, and 45 percent of our children live in low-income families, "the way we see the world," Glaude writes, "has gone out of whack." "The top 1 percent keep getting richer, while working people of all races have seen their wages stagnate; many have lost their jobs, their homes, and any hope that they might bequeath to their children a brighter future."[6] Particularly in Black communities, effort after effort is frustrated within these systems where failure feels inevitable. As the men in the prison have told me, "Growing up, I had to choose between the best of bad options."

This frustration and failure lead to a sense of nihilism in Black communities—a lived experience of meaninglessness, hopelessness, and lovelessness. Cornel West writes that the result of this nihilism is a numb detachment from others and a self-destructive disposition toward the world. It resembles a kind of collective clinical depression. People need to believe there is hope for the future, that their struggle will be worthwhile and meaningful.[7] People must be able to affirm their own worth and have opportunities to contribute to their families and their communities. People must know they matter in order for the threat of nihilism to be tamed.

✂

A week after I had cut DeShawn off in class, I returned to teach again. As usual, DeShawn arrived early, and I recognized the opportunity to apologize.

"DeShawn, I'm glad you're here early. I wanted to say I'm sorry for the way I cut you off in class last week. You were headed in a direction I didn't expect the discussion to go, a direction I wasn't prepared for. But you weren't wrong, DeShawn."

DeShawn bowed his head. "Oh, that's OK. But thank you." He smiled.

The other men arrived soon after this brief exchange, class began, and I didn't think of the conversation again. DeShawn must have, though, because he brought it back up again after the class ended. He approached me, hesitantly.

"Uh, Reverend Ott," he began.

"Yes, DeShawn?"

"I just wanted to say thank you for what you said earlier. Thank you. I really appreciated that."

"Oh. Of course," I said as we shook hands, something passing between us that's hard to explain, like respect or appreciation.

From then on, DeShawn leaned further into our class discussions, asserted himself when the conversation got off track, and helped keep the other guys focused on where I was trying to lead them. He made it easier for me as a teacher, and I felt myself growing more confident, less anxious. I joked around more and became more flexible, less tied to the agenda I brought to the class, more open to the unexpected epiphanies and learning possibilities for both students and teachers.

Each night, as class ended and the guard arrived to escort the men back to their cells, emotion gripped my chest and threatened to leak from my eyes. I pictured DeShawn and the others returning to their cement cells with peeling paint, whereas I got to drive home to hug and cuddle my kids before slipping under my bed's soft cotton sheets and down comforter. Our class was full of men who had murdered, abused and sold drugs, stolen, and cheated. But it was hard for me to imagine them committing these crimes. Especially DeShawn. DeShawn with his boyish grin, so eager to please, my best student. I didn't want to disappoint them as their teacher. I didn't want to fail. But I knew I would.

On the last day of class, I passed out certificates of graduation that I had quickly created and printed at my office before coming. The certificates held no value—they were just pieces of paper. But to these men, they were a symbol of accomplishment. I called each man's name, and he came forward to accept his certificate amid applause, shouts of praise, and some celebrative dance moves. The men crowded me afterward to shake my hand and say goodbye. None of us expected to see one another again. DeShawn was the last to approach.

He clasped my right hand in a warm shake, smiled, and said simply, "Reverend Ott." Two other students, goofing off, interrupted us, shouting for my attention, but DeShawn shooed them away playfully. "Hey, guys, back off, I need a moment here." Then returning his attention to me, he repeated, "Reverend Ott." Then "Thank you."

I added my left hand to the top of our clasped right hands and smiled back at DeShawn.

"No. Thank you, DeShawn. Really. Thank you."

There are no fairy tale endings in justice work. I would fail—repeatedly—in my interactions with these men and as a volunteer in the prison system. My experiences had taught me this. But the tragedy, I've also learned, is not in failing but in not risking failure as a privileged person who has such a choice. Had I not risked failing, I would not have met DeShawn, would not have gotten to know the inner workings of our corrections system, would not have grown in understanding about the social systems the majority of our incarcerated people come from. My failures here have arrested me, laying me low to face the pain of my inadequacies and my mistakes of apathy as one of the protected privileged. In this arrested state, my soul works me over, forcing me to push up and out, to keep risking, to keep failing, to keep becoming a new and better person.

Suggested Action Steps to Risk Failing

1. Make a list of ten justice-oriented actions you would take if you knew you couldn't fail. Risk taking one action step toward one item on your list.

2. Reflect on a failure or a mistake you have made. How did it feel to make that mistake? How did you respond to the mistake? Write down a list of actions you can take that will "arrest" or stop you from avoiding your mistake. Journaling? Prayer? Conversation with a friend? Accountability partner?

3. Consider the large systemic issues in your community that need to be changed, reformed, or eradicated: poverty, homelessness, hunger, incarceration. Choose one issue and take one action that will get you closer to the people most affected. Apply to volunteer in your local social service agency or homeless shelter, volunteer to deliver food to impoverished homes in your community, call your local prison and ask how you can begin the process to become a volunteer.

Chapter Ten

Risk Succeeding

What I want and what I want from you run parallel—
justice and the openings for just us.

—CLAUDIA RANKINE, *Just Us: An American Conversation*

"Wear long pants and long sleeves," I told the seven students gathered in the meeting room outside my chaplain's office. Over the course of a full academic year, I had recruited these college students, emailed them, texted them, messaged them on social media to remind them to return their required background check forms and attend this meeting. It felt like a miracle that I had successfully arranged for my husband and me to take these students on a three-hour visit to the prison, including a tour and a two-hour class with some of the incarcerated men we had gotten to know. When I first started planning this trip, it spanned a whole week of visits to different prisons, prison education programs, and nonprofit reentry organizations. That trip fell apart as forms were lost or not submitted on time and as students backed out for one unforeseeable reason or another. All I was able to secure was this three-hour visit. Now any little thing—wearing the wrong clothes, forgetting an ID, losing a visitor pass, the prison going on lockdown—could cancel this experience too.

Since I'd first set foot in the prison, I'd wanted to take students there. My husband is a professor at the same college I served as chaplain, and we dreamed about teaching a class inside the prison, where our students and the incarcerated men could be colearners. But the warden had been opposed to the idea. In his mind, eighteen- to twenty-one-year-olds weren't mature enough for the prison environment. I'd agree with him, but our criminal justice system suggests otherwise. Nearly every day, the United States incarcerates about sixty thousand youth in juvenile facilities.[1] In 2017, over four thousand youth ages seventeen and younger were incarcerated in adult facilities.[2] And five states (Georgia, Michigan, Missouri, Texas, and Wisconsin) automatically prosecute seventeen-year-olds as adults.[3]

After a year and a half of coordinating a group of faculty volunteers, I'd banked enough trust and goodwill for the warden to cautiously approve my request for this student trip. Now I needed my students to understand what they needed to do to get us inside.

"Basically, be sure to be covered up. No low necklines. No shorts. No bra straps showing. Cover up any tattoos you might have. Don't wear blue."

"Why can't we wear blue?" Nia asked.

I glanced at my husband, Dan. *How much should we tell them?* I asked in my look. I didn't want to scare anyone, but spelling these things out was part of the educational experience.

Dan's better at sounding less anxious than me. "The prisoners wear blue, and basically, you don't want to be confused for one of them if something were to happen. But nothing's ever happened while we've been there, and we've been there many times."

I decided not to add any more. Our students didn't need to know how I look up at the guard towers every time I walk into the prison, watching the officers who stand guard with rifles watching me. The whole situation tempts me to wear fluorescent pink.

As we reviewed all the protocols for our prison visit, the students' faces were blank. They didn't seem as frightened to go to the prison as I had been two years ago.

Do NOT PICK UP HITCHHIKERS.

For six years I read this sign and kept driving. It wasn't just my fear that kept me from the prison; it was also the thought that I might succeed. At that point in my career, I was confident in my ability to build programs and meaningful ministries. I'd served three different churches as a pastor where I'd built a variety of programs, and my work at the college was going well. If I reached out to this prison, if I ventured into the need

I knew was behind those fences and walls, I might build a successful outreach program between my college and the prison that worked and made a difference. And then what?

The Haitian proverb "There are mountains beyond mountains" resonates deeply. The nature of justice work, the righting of societal wrongs, is never-ending. It's the kind of work that leads social workers to burn out and pastors to leave the ministry. You might successfully climb one mountain, only to discover another mountain to climb. To succeed in any kind of outreach to the prison would only lead to more needs and more work.

Just how much of me is required here? What will this cost me? How much must I sacrifice? my inner voice of privilege asks every time I weigh the risk of succeeding.

When our group arrived at the prison, my favorite guard was at the front gate. Officer Bryant was the friendliest guard I'd met. He didn't try to act tough like the others or make things harder than they had to be. The warden was waiting for us at the gate too. *Maybe this visit is really going to happen.*

We signed in, got our visitor badges, and had our hands stamped with an invisible ink we'd get checked under a fluorescent light by a guard farther back in the prison. I encouraged everyone to use the bathrooms here at the front gate because they were the cleanest. "Be sure to wash your hands!" I emphasized, like a germaphobic mom. After each of us walked through the metal detector—the kind used at the airport thirty years ago—and no red lights or buzzers went off, our group cheered.

The warden led us to the break room where roll call was taken every morning. "Here, the night shift informs the day shift of anything that happened that they need to know about."

As I listened, I noticed one of the students, Shanice, jump and clutch her hand to her mouth. Elena reached out to comfort her, rubbing Shanice's back.

I moved to Shanice's side. "Are you OK?" I asked, thinking she might feel panicky or claustrophobic now that we were farther into the prison.

"Yes, I'm OK," Shanice said weakly. "There was a rat in there."

"What?!" Now I was freaking.

"It ran across the wall and went behind the vending machine." Shanice took some deep breaths.

Dan overheard us. "Oh, yeah, I've seen mice in here before."

The rat sighting left us full of nervous giggles. But as the warden proceeded to lead us through the final heavy metal door separating us from the incarcerated men, our group, full of young people not mature enough for prison, grew quiet and serious.

We were led into the large outdoor yard that connects all the cell blocks. Units of incarcerated men were escorted through here to get to the dining hall. As our group of casually dressed college students emerged onto the yard, the incarcerated men were halted to give us room to pass safely by—their eyes following us like we were the colorful new betta in the fishbowl.

"Don't get yourself locked up in prison, kids," one man called.

✣

I didn't expect to reform our criminal justice system by volunteering at my prison. I did expect to learn more about the eighteen hundred men incarcerated fifteen miles from my home. But was that enough?

One of the ways privileged people excuse themselves from risking success is by living in our heads. We can rationalize our way out of any risk to which our heart calls us.

In Luke 10, Jesus tells the parable of the Good Samaritan to interpret what it means to love "your neighbor as yourself." On the road from Jerusalem to Jericho, a man falls into the hands of robbers and is stripped, beaten, and left for dead. A priest happens by and sees the wounded man but passes by with, I'm sure, legitimate, rational reasons why he shouldn't stop. Maybe he's too busy with other important, godly work. If he stops to help this man, he won't be able to help those waiting for him down the road. Next, a Levite passes the wounded man, probably with his own reasons. Maybe the robbers are still around and this is a trap; if he stops to help that man, will he be ambushed? He won't be good to anyone if he gets hurt. Finally, a Samaritan arrives on the scene, and, Luke says, "he was moved with pity." A more literal translation of the Greek is "his heart was melting."

Privilege, according to Claudia Rankine, is not feeling touched by events that don't interfere with your reality.[4] In order to risk succeeding, in order to be a part of the liberating work our society needs, we must be open and willing to respond to the call of our heart. We privileged people must be liberated from the fears and rationalizations that keep us from stopping, pausing, disrupting the "normal" of our lives in order to reach out to our neighbors. Liberation theologian Gustavo Gutiérrez writes that justice work requires us to love as people of flesh and blood, to love with hearts that melt when we encounter neighbors who are in need. Liberation, Gutiérrez writes, will not come from cold religious obligation or a charitable sense of duty. It will come not from mechanical rationalizations of our mind but from authentic, fleshy, heart connections.[5] God works among us, freeing us, opening our hearts, helping us become more fully human, or humane, through the relationships that grow between neighbors who need the liberation each can offer the other.

Claudia Rankine writes, "What I want and what I want from you run parallel—justice and the openings for just us."[6] Rankine doesn't ask for anything unreasonable. I find her writing—a mix of academic research, artistic images, poetry, and prose—inspiring. At the beginning of her book *Just Us: An American Conversation*, she gives herself an assignment: converse with people she doesn't normally speak to, create liminal spaces through the complicated mess of true conversation. As a Black woman who teaches a class on Whiteness at Yale University, she is particularly interested in speaking to White men. She feels certain that as a Black woman, there has to be something she doesn't understand about White privilege. Throughout the book, she details her attempts (some successful, some failed) at conversations with White men in airport lounges, at gates, on planes. She holds back from statements that feel too sharp in order to keep the conversation going. She listens. But she also questions herself and the man with whom she is speaking. She refuses to simplify, stereotype, reduce, or dehumanize. Her goal, through these conversations, is to disrupt the distance between us, to "jam the machinery"[7] of our "strategies of silence, refusal of discomfort, willful blindness, and rage that cancels the complexity of response,"[8] to debunk racial myths and deconstruct racial fantasies, to make space for what might be possible between us, to allow our hearts to melt.

The warden apologized that he couldn't show us an actual cell, but he walked us into the main guard post at the hub of a cell block shaped like a large X. From the bulletproof-glassed booth in the middle of the X, we could see down each hallway of the two-story cell block. White halls, white doors with a small window in each. Some men were milling about in the hallway, but most, I assumed, were behind their cell doors. I was struck by the lack of color, the metal staircases leading from one story of cells to the other, the peeling paint. It looked more like the mental institution in *One Flew over the Cuckoo's Nest*. Seeing this, I understood better why the men who attended our classes were so eager to get out of their cells.

The warden introduced us to the three guards working that cell block. "They've got a tough job," he said. "They've got to make sure they know what is happening on each of these hallways at all times and where each man is." Then he added,

"This is all about control—which is hard. I mean, just think if you were to be stuck in a room that size with your brother or sister. Fights break out all the time."

"I heard the flu was going around," I said to the warden.

"Yes," he responded, "it's pretty bad right now."

"How do you isolate a virus like that in prison? Do you pull the men from their cells and put them in the infirmary?"

"No," he responded. "We isolate their cell and the two cells next to their cell and move the other men away."

"Do you pull their cellie out?"

"No. We just isolate their cell."

So, I thought to myself, *if your cellie gets the flu, you're screwed because you're going to get it too.*

Earlier, during our previsit meeting, Dan shared with our students that the men love coming to our classes because it's the only time they are treated like human beings. "In prison, they're treated like a number or a thing that needs to be controlled," Dan said. "And they very much feel that."

Cornel West calls on progressives to take seriously issues of Black identity or the uncritical acceptance of self-degrading ideals that question Black intelligence, possibility, and beauty. Black poverty must be addressed, West writes, through both the redistributive efforts of affirmative action and "human affirmative efforts." Those who feel less than human or are treated as less than human need to be humanized.

Rankine's work seeks to meet this humanizing need. She opens space for us to encounter the humanity of the racial other, the stranger, the beaten man on the side of the road—to engage the person whose life and struggles don't interfere with our reality. In her book *Don't Let Me Be Lonely,* she writes about her sadness that lives—particularly Black lives—never mattered. She illustrates this with a photograph of James Byrd Jr. and the account of his beating in rural East Texas. In 1998, John King, Lawrence Brewer, and Shawn Berry beat, chained, and then dragged Byrd from the back of their pickup truck. Another photograph shows the spot on the asphalt where Byrd's decapitated head was found. "My sadness is alive," Rankine writes, "alongside the recognition that billions of lives never mattered. I write this without breaking my heart, without bursting into anything. Perhaps this is the real source of my sadness. Cornel West says this is what is wrong with black people today—too nihilistic. Too scarred by hope to hope, too experienced to experience, too close to dead is what I think."[9]

After the tour, the warden dropped us off in one of the vocational building's classrooms, where we would wait for the men to join us. I'd been in this classroom before and preferred it to some of the others. It was smaller, with scuffed red institutional carpet on the floor. The school desks, old and beat up, were a hodgepodge of various sizes. Our students chose desks for themselves, gravitating toward the sturdier, larger ones. I suddenly pictured the six adult men who would soon join us, many over six feet tall, squeezing into the smaller remaining desks, perhaps donated from a junior high. I panicked at our inhospitality and was about to tell the students to move, but it was too late.

DeShawn entered the classroom first. I stood by the classroom door to welcome the men after they checked in with the guard outside. I wanted to tell each of them how happy I was that they could participate in this special class and help them feel more comfortable entering this room full of strangers. I cringed as DeShawn bent his long frame to fit into one of the tiny available desks. Then Turell arrived. Jarek. Hareem. They trickled in, since they were arriving from different cell blocks. Chad. And finally, Terrance.

When Terrance opened the door to our classroom, I greeted him with an "Oh, good! You made it!" I'd just gotten to know Terrance, but I'd added him to the class because I was worried some of the other men would be out with the flu.

He nodded. "Thank you for inviting me. I really appreciate it."

"Of course. I'm thrilled you are here. Did you have time to do the reading?" He must have gotten it only the day before.

"Yes, I did. Thank you."

After I greeted each of the men at the door, they systematically moved to each student in the room and my husband, shaking each hand and politely saying hello before sitting down.

Dan got the class started with an introduction to James Baldwin's short story "Sonny's Blues." He'd chosen this story because he'd taught it in another prison class and thought it would be a great way to connect the experiences of our students (many of whom came from urban Chicago neighborhoods) to the men who were incarcerated. The story focuses on two brothers from Harlem trying to make sense of their lives. One becomes a jazz musician who is, in Baldwin's words, "trying to work out his salvation at the piano." He ends up getting addicted to heroin and going to prison. His brother chooses the straight-and-narrow path: he goes into the military and becomes a teacher but distances himself emotionally from his family and life.

Our college students were hesitant to speak at first. It's intimidating to be in a classroom full of adult men dressed in blue scrubs. There's no escaping that you're in a prison. But the conversation quickly warmed. Jarek and Hareem, who had started a mentoring program in the prison, kept reaching out to Trevon and Andre, asking them to share their thoughts. Trevon and Andre got comfortable quickly and even tossed good-natured barbs about fading hairlines and Jarek's bald head. Turell and DeShawn interjected every once in a while with nuggets of wisdom and coaxed Nia, Elena, and Shanice out of their shyness, calling, "Hey, what do you think about this?"

Terrance, it turned out, had not only read the story but had read it so carefully that he kept returning us to lines we hadn't noticed or recalled on our own. Before we knew it, we were bantering thoughts back and forth, laughing and listening.

The guard rapped on the classroom door, our two hours of class time at an end before we were ready to let one another go. As the men filed out, they paused again to shake each of our hands and thank us for coming.

I've never been in a context where a handshake is taken more seriously than the prison. It's the only form of touch allowed between prisoner and visitor, and the men insist on shaking all hands before and after each class.

Next to a photo of a large billboard that reads simply "Here" in big, bold letters, Rankine writes about the handshake as our ritual of both asserting that I am here and handing ourselves over to another. Here. Take this. Take me. It's an offering of presence, Rankine writes. It both recognizes and demands recognition. "In order for something to be handed over a hand must extend and a hand must receive. We must both be here in this world in this life in this place."[10]

Here. Shake my hand. Human to human.

On the van ride home, Dan was driving, so I could turn around in the passenger seat to talk to the students. "OK, what'd you think?"

"That was amazing," Nia responded immediately.

The rest of the group agreed.

I smiled at their enthusiasm. "What'd you think of the men?"

"I thought Jarek was very bold," Andre shared. "He talked about heroin as an escape when we discussed Sonny going there in the story."

Elena jumped in. "I liked Turell. He was really wise."

Trevon said, "Andre and I just felt like we were with some of our older uncles chillin' at a barbecue. Throwing a little shade about going bald."

"What'd you think of Terrance?" I asked. "I added him at the last minute, so he got the short story the day before the class, and he read it so carefully."

"Yeah," Andre added. "He kept taking us back to the text. He was like, 'Now on page seventy-seven . . .'" We laughed.

Shanice said, "I liked how they were able to connect the story to their lives and to our lives. Like there wasn't a big disconnect between us. They'd say how the story related to them, but then say, 'But you as a college student or you as a young person might hear this . . .'"

The conversation paused for a moment as we collectively contemplated the experience we'd all just shared. Elena finally broke in: "Did anyone else think Hareem looked like Common?"

Laughter broke us open—wild and free—as we drove through the dark, down the highway, past the prison. The past three hours weren't what I'd originally envisioned for this educational trip. We might have grown in awareness, but we made no progress toward the complex reforms our criminal justice system needs. But successes, even small ones, ought to be celebrated. Riding home that night in that van, I couldn't stop smiling. My heart felt large and full and melted in my chest.

Suggested Action Steps to Risk Succeeding

1. What problems in your community don't interfere with your life? Homelessness? Hunger?

LGBTQ+ rights? Make one small change in
your routine this week so your path will cross
that of a person struggling with one of these
problems. Take a walk through an impoverished
neighborhood. Visit the local LGBTQ+ hangout.
Read a novel about a people struggling with
famine, like Imbolo Mbue's *How Beautiful We Were*,
then volunteer to help serve a meal at your local
shelter.

2. What social justice work have you not gotten
   involved in because you believed it would
   require too much of you? That you would have
   to sacrifice too much? Say yes to one request
   or one aspect of that justice work. Volunteer
   at one event. March in one protest. Knock on
   doors one afternoon to advocate for a political
   candidate. Write one letter or one email to
   a local, state, or national political leader.
   Compose a blog or social media post about
   what you learned or how you benefited from
   this action.

3. For one week, take on the spiritual practice of
   speaking to strangers. Like Claudia Rankine,
   seek opportunities to converse with people you
   don't normally speak to—the post office clerk, a
   man you've noticed seeking shelter at the public
   library, the older woman eating breakfast alone
   at McDonald's. Offer these strangers your time

and presence, and be attentive to what unfolds between you. Journal about these interactions afterward. What did you learn? What did you feel? How did your body respond in these moments of connection?

Conclusion

La vida es la lucha—the struggle is life.

—ADA MARÍA ISASI-DÍAZ, *Mujerista Theology*

I am a different person from who I was when I began writing this book.

I am less afraid to take necessary risks. In fact, I feel compelled to take more risks, inspired to place myself in conversations and contexts that will challenge my assumptions, biases, and prejudices. I am more culturally competent, more capable of negotiating conversations across boundaries and borders of difference. I am more resilient. Less fragile. I bounce back quicker from mistakes. I stay with discomfort and tension longer than I ever would have before. My heart is more willing, more open, less likely to hold hard certainties, less tempted to dominate, control, or win.

I am more aware of the Whiteness that dominates all our lives. In the room where the portraits of my college's past presidents hang, I notice that they are all White men, except for one White woman. At an impromptu demonstration on the college's front lawn, I observe that the students gathered are predominantly White. *Where are the students of color? I wonder. Why aren't they participating? How can I find out what they think about this demonstration?* As I flip through the pages of a magazine, I note that the contributing writers, as well as the authors of the sources they cite, are predominantly White. I am more appreciative—hungry, even—for diversity.

When I began writing this book, I did not know where the journey would lead me; I didn't understand or know the goal. But I am better for having gone to the prison, to the Black students' table in the dining hall, to the living room full of mujeristas. I feel freer. More flexible. Opportunities and possibilities feel more abundant.

According to Ada María Isasi-Díaz, mujeristas commonly respond to the casual "How are you?" with *"Ahí, en la lucha"* (There, in the struggle). This could be heard as only a nod to the specific suffering of Latin women, the oppression and historic injustices they must daily endure. But, Isasi-Díaz writes, the focus of *la lucha* is not their suffering but their struggle for liberation: "All we need to ask of God is to have health and strength to struggle. The struggle is my life; my dedication to the struggle is one of the main driving forces in my life."[1] To focus only on their suffering would suggest Latina women see themselves as subjects acted upon by their oppressors. Instead, mujeristas are agents of their own destiny, locating themselves in *la lucha*, aware of the role they play in defining and bringing about a better, more secure future for us all.[2]

Conclusion

Before I met and came to know Jocelyn, I assumed I didn't have much to offer the students of color at my college. Like the big kid sidelined in the game red rover so no one got hurt, my insecurity led me to believe my White privilege and ignorance of their reality disqualified me from being their chaplain. But I had underestimated the role of being a willing listener to a young person seeking to understand herself and her world. I had also underestimated the power of placing the right book in the right hands.

After I introduced Jocelyn to *Mujerista Theology*, she couldn't keep it to herself. We decided to start a special study group for Latina students on campus. We debated the makeup of the group—whether it should be all Latinas, or Latinas and other students of color, or Latinas and other allies. Just as Isasi-Díaz came to realize that Latin women needed a theology separate from liberationists and White feminists, Jocelyn and I concluded that the Latina students on our campus needed this space for themselves. Curious to see what this group would become, I had hoped to attend every meeting. Instead, I resigned myself to visiting only occasionally.

Jocelyn began recruiting and quickly had fourteen Latinas committed to the study group. They were not all Christians. As Jocelyn described it, the group included an atheist, a few strong Catholics, some spiritual-but-not-religious types, a Protestant, and one who was searching for faith. All were drawn, though, to the study of theology written by a Brown woman like them.

When I visited the group, I was tempted to take over and facilitate. These young Latina women had never studied

187

theology, and I could have taken them deeper into the text. But a White woman taking the lead would run counter to Isasi-Díaz's purposes. My place was to empower these Latina students to ask their own questions and use me as a sounding board to practice articulating what they were learning.

The way those budding mujeristas welcomed me was not something I took lightly. Trust was not a given in that circle. According to Jocelyn, three of the young women were undocumented, two having registered through President Obama's DACA program.

For each meeting, Jocelyn prepared a handout with questions for the group to consider. As I read over the sheet she handed me, I paused to take in this paragraph: "Isasi-Díaz states, 'If there is not mutuality among the oppressed, they can very easily become tomorrow's oppressors.' What do you think this means? As the Latinx population continues to grow, it is expected that our community will be a majority in 2050. What sort of implications does this have for us as Latinas that advocate for justice? What is our responsibility to the rest of the world?"

I was struck by the grace of the question, knowing that these young Latinas were angry and upset after the 2016 presidential election and the anti-immigrant rhetoric it inflamed. I also felt a hint of relief, unaware until that moment of a subtle, nagging fear. Fear of my privilege and power being torn down like a Confederate statue. Fear of losing what I had achieved as a woman working in a male-dominated field. Fear of change that would make struggle *my* life.

Yet here were fourteen Latina women contemplating how they will care for the world when they become the ones with power and privilege. As they bantered in Spanish and English, leaning into one another, their brown eyes full of empathy and compassion, their heads nodding support, I sat quietly to take them in. *Yes*, I thought to myself, *I'd be OK with these women being the ones in charge.* Wisdom surrounded them—a wisdom I did not know but could feel like a physical presence. As they each testified to their struggle, life itself was held like a precious jewel in the room.

Andrea said, "I can't wait for the day when we're not under this pressure to change ourselves."

Maria added, "I'm tired of the message 'You can't do this. You can't have that.'"

Belinda spoke about her White roommate, who didn't like her Latin music, part of the soul of her culture: "My brother came to pick me up in his car, and he was cranking his music, and she looked at him so weird. I just got in the car and bawled. Why am I hiding and adjusting myself for a society that doesn't want me? Why can't I listen to my music?"

Jocelyn, sitting back in her chair, elbows on the armrests, hands clasped thoughtfully before her mouth, said, "Sometimes I think about going back to Mexico. *¿Me entiendes?* But I have new knowledge. I can't just forget everything and go there. There's stuff to do here."

These Latina students were growing in solidarity and reflection, finding within themselves and their shared stories the resources needed to continue in *la lucha*.

In this circle, in this struggle, I have come to realize that I am not excluded. I have come to trust that the struggle is for the liberation of us all.

"Latinas are not separatist," Isasi-Díaz writes, "we do not exclude others from ourselves and from *la lucha*, nor do we struggle exclusively for ourselves. If we succeed in the present system, it will be because someone else takes our place at the bottom of the socioeconomic-political ladder."[3] Together, in community and in solidarity, mujeristas overcome the temptation to free themselves from oppression at the expense of those they leave behind.

What these Latinas know, what my privilege and my fears have kept me from understanding, is that in the long run, what benefits all of humanity benefits me as well. Liberation theology often confronts the privileged with the uncomfortable truth that we don't know we need to be saved, that we don't know the needs of our own souls, that we don't know how we would benefit from a world with more just systems and structures. If we are not dying from hunger or poverty or systemic racism, our privilege veils our need. The dehumanizing systems we benefit from separate us as people, harden the borders between us, and keep us from opportunities for transformation and growth. We privileged people can begin to understand this when we risk venturing into spaces where we cannot dominate, where we can meet and come to know people whose lives are culturally, economically, and politically different from our own.

"*La vida es la lucha*—the struggle is life." I remember discussing this quote with Jocelyn. Isasi-Díaz uses it like a mantra or a call to action.

"Doesn't this literally translate as 'Life is struggle' instead of 'The struggle is life'?" I asked, my undergraduate degree in Spanish kicking in.

"Yeah," Jocelyn responded. "But that's not what she means."

Jocelyn intuited Isasi-Díaz's meaning long before I began to catch on. It took a lot of necessary risk taking for me to begin to understand. Life itself may be a struggle for Latina women and many marginalized peoples, but it is not *the* struggle to which Isasi-Díaz calls us. *The* struggle is the struggle of our lives and for our lives. *The* struggle includes suffering, but it is not about the suffering. *The* struggle is the effort we put into the sacred work of liberating people and communities and countries from oppression.

I hope, dear reader, that you hear an invitation to the struggle through this book, which is also an invitation to life. It's an invitation for privileged people to move beyond fear, to take necessary risks, to heal and free our souls. The struggle is life and life giving. The more we privileged people embrace this truth and its necessary risks, the more we can participate in the liberation of us all.

Notes

Introduction: On Fear

1 Susan Nelson Dunfee, "The Sin of Hiding: A Feminist Critique of Reinhold Niebuhr's Account of the Sin of Pride," *Soundings: An Interdisciplinary Journal* 65, no. 3 (Fall 1982): 325.

2 Martin Luther King Jr., "Antidotes to Fear," in *A Testament of Hope: The Essential Writings and Speeches of Martin Luther King, Jr.*, ed. James M. Washington (New York: HarperCollins, 1986), 510–11.

3 Resmaa Menakem, *My Grandmother's Hands: Racialized Trauma and the Pathway to Mending Our Hearts and Bodies* (Las Vegas: Central Recovery, 2017), 7.

4 Menakem, 15.

5 bell hooks, *Teaching to Transgress: Education as the Practice of Freedom* (New York: Routledge, 1994), 26.

Chapter One: Risk Going

1 Chris Hoke, "Exchanging Letters with People in Hell," *Christian Century*, October 26, 2016, 24.

Notes

2 Beverly Daniel Tatum, *Why Are All the Black Kids Sitting Together in the Cafeteria? And Other Conversations about Race* (1997; repr., New York: Basic, 2017), 134.

3 Shannon Sullivan, *Revealing Whiteness: The Unconscious Habits of Racial Privilege* (Bloomington: Indiana University Press, 2006), 25.

4 Sullivan, 150–51, 122.

5 Paulo Freire, *Pedagogy of the Oppressed* (New York: Bloomsbury Academic, 1970), 49.

6 Bryan Stevenson, "We're Taking the Wrong Approach to Criminal Justice Reform," *Time*, February 24, 2020, https://time.com/5783965/bryan-stevenson-criminal-justice-reform/.

7 Gloria Anzaldúa, *Borderlands / La Frontera: The New Mestiza*, 4th ed. (San Francisco: Aunt Lute, 2012), 216.

8 Norma Elia Cantu and Aida Hurtado, "Breaking Borders / Constructing Bridges: Twenty-Five Years of *Borderlands / La Frontera*," in Anzaldúa, *Borderlands / La Frontera*, 5.

9 Anzaldúa, *Borderlands / La Frontera*, 108.

10 Anzaldúa, 28.

11 Anzaldúa, 100–101.

12 Anzaldúa, 70.

13 Anzaldúa, "Preface to the First Edition," in *Borderlands / La Frontera*, 21.

Chapter Two: Risk Staying

1 John McWorter, "The Dehumanizing Condescension of *White Fragility*," *Atlantic*, July 15, 2020, https://www.theatlantic.com/ideas/archive/2020/07/dehumanizing-condescension-white-fragility/614146/.

2 Jennifer Loubriel, "4 Ways White People Can Process Their Emotions without Bringing the White Tears," Everyday

Notes

Feminism, February 16, 2016, https://everydayfeminism.com/2016/02/white-people-emotions-tears/.

3 Audre Lorde, *Sister Outsider: Essays and Speeches by Audre Lorde* (New York: Crossing, 1984), 124.

4 Brené Brown, *Daring Greatly: How the Courage to Be Vulnerable Transforms the Way We Live, Love, Parent, and Lead* (New York: Penguin Random House, 2012), 68–69, 71.

5 Brown, 63.

6 Sullivan, *Revealing Whiteness*, 122.

7 Barbara Brown Taylor, *Leaving Church: A Memoir of Faith* (New York: HarperCollins, 2006), 146–47.

8 Brown, *Daring Greatly*, 67.

9 Ibram X. Kendi, *Stamped from the Beginning: The Definitive History of Racist Ideas in America* (New York: Nation, 2016), 3, 6.

10 Freire, *Pedagogy of the Oppressed*, 63.

11 Freire, 65.

12 Ada María Isasi-Díaz, *Mujerista Theology* (Maryknoll, NY: Orbis, 1996), 21–22.

13 Lorde, *Sister Outsider*, 57.

14 Lorde, 55.

15 Lorde, 58.

16 Brown, *Daring Greatly*, 64–65.

17 Lorde, *Sister Outsider*, 130.

Chapter Three: Risk Learning

1 Lorde, *Sister Outsider*, 113.

2 Debby Irving, *Waking Up White, and Finding Myself in the Story of Race* (Cambridge, MA: Elephant Room, 2014), 170.

3 James Baldwin, *Notes of a Native Son* (Boston: Beacon, 1955), 98.

4 Baldwin, 96.

5 Sullivan, *Revealing Whiteness*, 19–24.

Chapter Four: Risk Teaching

1 bell hooks, *Teaching Community: A Pedagogy of Hope* (New York: Routledge, 2003), 197.

2 Tony Judt, "Night," *New York Review of Books*, January 14, 2010, 4.

3 bell hooks, *All about Love: New Visions* (New York: HarperCollins, 2000), 93.

4 hooks, 90.

5 hooks, *Teaching Community*, 192.

6 hooks, 197.

7 hooks, 158.

Chapter Five: Risk Following

1 Marianne Schnall, "An Interview with Maya Angelou," *Psychology Today*, February 17, 2009, https://www.psychologytoday.com/us/blog/the-guest-room/200902/interview-maya-angelou.

2 Martin Luther King Jr., *Where Do We Go from Here: Chaos or Community?* (Boston: Beacon, 1968), 99.

3 "Selected Population Profile in the United States," Table S0201, American Community Survey, United States Census Bureau, https://data.census.gov/cedsci/table?t=002%20-%20White%20alone%3AAge%20and%20Sex&y=2016&tid=ACSSPP1Y2016.S0201&hidePreview=false.

4 Robin DiAngelo, *White Fragility: Why It's So Hard for White People to Talk about Racism* (Boston: Beacon, 2018), 31.

5 Freire, *Pedagogy of the Oppressed*, 60.

6 Saul Alinsky, *Rules for Radicals: A Pragmatic Primer for Realistic Radicals* (New York: Random House, 1971), 104.

7 Alinsky, 106.

8 Freire, *Pedagogy of the Oppressed*, 56.

9 Carolyn Forché, *What You Have Heard Is True: A Memoir of Witness and Resistance* (New York: Penguin, 2019), 384.

Chapter Six: Risk Leading

1 King, *Where Do We Go from Here*, 96.
2 Martin Luther King Jr., "Letter from Birmingham City Jail," in *Testament of Hope*, 295.
3 King, 291.
4 David J. Garrow, *Bearing the Cross: Martin Luther King Jr. and the Southern Christian Leadership Conference* (New York: Harper-Collins, 1986), 139.
5 King, *Where Do We Go from Here*, 136.
6 William J. Barber II, *The Third Reconstruction: How a Moral Movement Is Overcoming the Politics of Division and Fear* (Boston: Beacon, 2016), 50.
7 King, *Where Do We Go from Here*, 97.

Chapter Seven: Risk Listening

1 Adapted from W. E. B. Du Bois, *Dusk of Dawn: An Essay toward an Autobiography of a Race Concept* (New Brunswick, NJ: Transaction, 1984), 130–31.
2 James Baldwin, "As Much Truth as One Can Bear," in *The Cross of Redemption: Uncollected Writings*, ed. Randall Kenan (New York: Vintage, 2011), 33.
3 Ivan Natividad, "The Time James Baldwin Told UC Berkeley That Black Lives Matter," *Berkeley News*, June 19, 2020, https://news.berkeley.edu/2020/06/19/the-time-james-baldwin-told-uc-berkeley-that-black-lives-matter/.
4 "Responding to the Insurrection at the US Capital," Facing History and Ourselves, January 6, 2021, https://www.facinghistory

.org/educator-resources/current-events/responding-insurrection
-us-capitol.

5 Anna Marie Vigen, "To Hear and to Be Accountable: An Ethic
of White Listening," in *Disrupting White Supremacy from Within:
White People on What We Need to Do*, ed. Jennifer Harvey, Karin
A. Case, and Robin Hawley Gorsline (Cleveland, OH: Pilgrim,
2004), 234.

6 Lorde, *Sister Outsider*, 124–35.

7 Vigen, "To Hear and to Be Accountable," 223.

8 James Baldwin, *James Baldwin's Collected Essays* (New York: Literary Classics of the United States, 1998), 723.

Chapter Eight: Risk Speaking

1 In the 1990s, we used the word *homosexual*, which is now considered outdated and offensive—a loaded term with the ring of
judgment. When speaking scientifically or medically, *gay, lesbian, bisexual, queer, transgender, intersex, asexual,* and *heterosex-
ual* are the terms used to more accurately describe a person's
enduring physical, romantic, and/or emotional attraction
to members of the same and/or opposite sex. For more, see
https://www.glaad.org/reference/lgbtq.

2 Elie Wiesel, *Night* (1958; repr., New York: Hill & Wang, 1986), 131.

3 Martin Luther King Jr., "A Time to Break Silence," *Testament of
Hope*, 231.

4 Garrow, *Bearing the Cross*, 543.

5 Jack Rogers, *Jesus, the Bible, and Homosexuality: Explode the Myths,
Heal the Church* (Louisville, KY: Westminster John Knox, 2006),
12.

6 Marion L. Soards, *Scripture and Homosexuality: Biblical Authority
and the Church Today* (Louisville, KY: Westminster John Knox,
1995), 16.

7 Garrow, *Bearing the Cross*, 554.

8 Garrow, 558.

9 Garrow, 554.

10 Garrow, 461.

11 Garrow, 560.

Chapter Nine: Risk Failing

1 Anzaldúa, *Borderlands / La Frontera*, 67.

2 Anzaldúa, 68.

3 Anzaldúa, 70.

4 King, *Where Do We Go from Here*, 122.

5 Eddie S. Glaude Jr., *Democracy in Black: How Race Still Enslaves the American Soul* (New York: Crown, 2016), 201.

6 Glaude, 203.

7 Cornel West, *Race Matters* (1993; repr., Boston: Beacon, 2017), 14–18.

Chapter Ten: Risk Succeeding

1 "America's Addiction to Juvenile Incarceration: State by State," American Civil Liberties Union, access date April 2021, https://www.aclu.org/issues/juvenile-justice/youth-incarceration/americas-addiction-juvenile-incarceration-state-state.

2 "Easy Access to the Census of Juveniles in Residential Placement," cited by Peter Wagner and Wanda Bertram, "'What Percent of the U.S. Is Incarcerated?' (And Other Ways to Measure Mass Incarceration)," Prison Policy Initiative, January 16, 2020, https://www.prisonpolicy.org/blog/2020/01/16/percent-incarcerated/.

3 "Despite Improvements, an Ineffective and Biased System Remains," Children's Defense Fund, accessed July 14, 2021,

https://www.childrensdefense.org/policy/resources/soac
-2020-youth-justice/.

4 Claudia Rankine, *Just Us: An American Conversation* (Minneapolis: Graywolf, 2020), 55.

5 Gustavo Gutiérrez, *A Theology of Liberation* (Maryknoll, NY: Orbis, 1988), 114.

6 Rankine, *Just Us*, 11.

7 Rankine, 329.

8 Rankine, 334.

9 Claudia Rankine, *Don't Let Me Be Lonely: An American Lyric* (Minneapolis: Graywolf, 2004), 23.

10 Rankine, 130–31.

Conclusion

1 Isasi-Díaz, *Mujerista Theology*, 22.

2 Ada María Isasi-Díaz, *En la Lucha: Elaborating a Mujerista Theology* (Minneapolis: Fortress, 2004), 178.

3 Isasi-Díaz, 59.

Recommended Resources

Getting Started

Acho, Emmanuel. *Uncomfortable Conversations with a Black Man.* New York: Flatiron, 2020.

Despite the title, Acho is a comfortable person to be in conversation with over uncomfortable issues. He addresses many of the questions White people have about Black people and Black culture but are afraid to ask. He explains concepts in a way that is easy to understand.

Harvey, Jennifer. *Raising White Kids.* Nashville: Abingdon, 2017.

Jennifer Harvey is a professor of religion at Drake University who has written extensively on racial justice and White antiracism. *Raising White Kids* is perhaps her most accessible book. It's a good read for White parents who want to raise antiracist children but also for all White people interested in exploring their own childhood and upbringing in our dominant White culture.

Irving, Debby. *Waking Up White, and Finding Myself in the Story of Race.* Cambridge, MA: Elephant Room, 2014.

Debby Irving's book is a wonderful introduction for White people who don't understand that they are White, what White culture is, and why it matters that White people understand their particular racial identity. The notes on sources at the end of the book are chock-full of great information. Irving's website also offers great resources and information: www.debbyirving.com.

Oluo, Ijeoma. *So You Want to Talk about Race*. New York: Seal, 2018.

Oluo also addresses many of the questions White people have about Black people and Black culture but from a Black woman's perspective. She also includes tips at the end of the book on how to move beyond "just talking" to actively helping create real change in the fight against racial oppression.

Stevenson, Bryan. *Just Mercy: A Story of Justice and Redemption*. New York: Spiegel & Grau, 2014.

If you're interested in learning about the racial injustices within our criminal justice system, Bryan Stevenson's book (and now the movie, starring Michael B. Jordan) is a must read. Also be sure to check out and support Stevenson's important work through the Equal Justice Initiative at https://eji.org.

Tatum, Beverly. *Why Are All the Black Kids Sitting Together in the Cafeteria? And Other Conversations about Race*. 1997. Reprint, New York: Basic, 2017.

Tatum recently published a twentieth-anniversary edition of this book, first published in 1997. She revised and updated the original, which still serves as an excellent primer for anyone wanting to learn about the dynamics of race in America. Tatum is especially helpful in understanding racial identity development in children, adolescents, and adults.

Going Deeper

Anzaldúa, Gloria. *Borderlands / La Frontera: The New Mestiza*. 4th ed. San Francisco: Aunt Lute, 2012.

As a queer, Chicana, feminist writer, Anzaldúa's thoughtful, creative work is important for those who have spent the majority of their lives separated from anyone or any way deemed "different" by the dominant majority. Her work highlights the growth and hope that comes when we risk crossing borders of our own making.

Baldwin, James. *Notes of a Native Son.* 1955. Reprint, Boston: Beacon, 1983.

I recommend all of James Baldwin's books. *Notes of a Native Son* was the first book of Baldwin's I read and an amazing introduction to his work. I also find Baldwin's fiction captivating. No matter where you choose to start with Baldwin, just start. You won't regret it.

Glaude, Eddie, Jr. *Begin Again: James Baldwin's America and Its Urgent Lessons for Our Own.* New York: Crown, 2020.

This book is an informative and influential conversation between two thinkers I deeply admire, James Baldwin and Eddie Glaude Jr. It's an excellent introduction to James Baldwin's work and his continued relevance today.

Haley, Alex. *The Autobiography of Malcolm X.* 1964. Reprint, New York: Ballantine, 1965.

Anyone interested in learning more about the Black experience in America should read about Malcolm X, whose thinking, leadership, and influence are often misconstrued. This book is the best introduction to Malcolm X.

hooks, bell. *All about Love: New Visions.* New York: HarperCollins, 2000.

bell hooks is a prolific writer, a master teacher, a Black feminist, and a thought leader who should be known and read widely. Her pen name, bell hooks, is not capitalized to shift attention from her identity to her ideas. Although her breakout book was *Ain't I a Woman: Black Women and Feminism*, I recommend *All about Love: New Visions* as an accessible entry point into all of hooks's work that is grounded in a love ethic.

Kendi, Ibram X. *How to Be an Antiracist*. New York: One World, 2019.

Kendi is an increasingly influential voice in the antiracist movement and important to read. I appreciate Kendi's willingness to be vulnerable and to honestly share how he has struggled to overcome his own racism, homophobia, and misogyny.

King, Martin Luther, Jr. *Where Do We Go from Here: Chaos or Community?* Boston: Beacon, 1968.

King wrote this book in 1967, but it reads like it was written today. Americans should move beyond the often-quoted sound bites of King and read him whole. This book is an excellent and informative dive into King's faith and thinking. His concluding vision for our "world house" is worth reading to the end.

Lorde, Audre. *Sister Outsider: Essays and Speeches by Audre Lorde*. 1984. Reprint, Berkeley, CA: Crossing, 2007.

If you want to familiarize yourself with Audre Lorde's work, this is the book to read. Each essay is full of profound insights and challenges to unjust status quos. Lorde is a force, and she is brilliant.

Menakem, Resmaa. *My Grandmother's Hands: Racialized Trauma and the Pathway to Mending Our Hearts and Bodies*. Las Vegas: Central Recovery, 2017.

Menakem calls us to recognize that racism is habituated not only in the mind but also in our bodies. Menakem's work on the generational trauma of American racism is fascinating and important. His book includes a variety of meditation activities to help us explore our pain and trauma and work toward healing. Menakem also offers more helpful resources for education and healing on his website: https://www.resmaa.com.

Sullivan, Shannon. *White Privilege*. Medford, MA: Polity, 2019.
This is the most accessible of Sullivan's books (she's a professor of philosophy) and a very thoughtful assessment of the advantages and disadvantages of the term *White privilege*.

West, Cornel. *Race Matters*. 1993. Reprint, Boston: Beacon, 2017.
Cornel West is a prolific intellectual and one of America's most important prophetic voices on issues of race. *Race Matters* is so influential that it's been republished three times and is still relevant beyond its twenty-five-year anniversary.

Liberation Theology

Cone, James H. *Said I Wasn't Gonna Tell Nobody*. Maryknoll, NY: Orbis, 2018.
I loved reading this memoir by the founder of Black liberation theology. After being thoroughly steeped in the systematic theology of White male traditionalists, Cone craved a way of thinking about God that embraced Blackness and the Black Power movement. Heading into his doctoral work in 1968, Cone believed that the time had come for Black people to stop consulting White theologians for the meaning of the Christian gospel. He wrote his first book, *Black Theology and Black Power*, while listening to the music of Mahalia Jackson, B. B. King, and Aretha Franklin.

Gutiérrez, Gustavo. *A Theology of Liberation*. 1973. Reprint, Maryknoll, NY: Orbis, 1988.
This is one of the defining books of Latin American liberation theology, which emerged in the 1960s after the Second Vatican Council and was popularized by Gustavo Gutiérrez, a

Dominican priest and theologian from Peru. Prioritizing concern for the poor and political liberation for the oppressed, liberation theology has spread across the globe and led the church to an ever-expanding conversation with Black, Hispanic, and Amerindian theologies as well as with those who have engaged in what Gutiérrez names "the especially fruitful thinking" of the feminist perspective.

Isasi-Díaz, Ada María. *Mujerista Theology*. Maryknoll, NY: Orbis, 1996.

Mujerista theology was developed by Ada María Isasi-Díaz with the goal of taking the religious understandings and practices of Latinas seriously. Isasi-Díaz challenges understandings, church teachings, and religious practices that oppress Latina women, are not life giving, and therefore, are not theologically correct. Anyone interested in Christian theology would be well served to study with the mujeristas.